VIRAT

Neeraj Jha is a television journalist, show producer, live sports broadcaster, writer and photographer with 19 years of experience in working across different departments and countries, and in-depth knowledge of producing live sports broadcasts. After passing out from the Indian Institute of Mass Communication (IIMC), he joined the International Management Group (IMG) and Trans World International (TWI), followed by working with media giants such as ETV Network and Zee Media Ltd. He joined Ten Sports in 2005 and worked there for 12 years. In 2017, he started his own company, Pixpo Media. A regular on TV, radio and digital media as a sports expert, he also writes articles for leading newspapers and digital platforms.

Vidhanshu Kumar has worked in all forms of media: print, TV, radio, online, and news agencies. Beginning with *Asian Age*, he moved on to TV, working with Sahara Samay, IBN 7 and News X channels. He reported on cricket from over 30 countries, as one of India's first few TV journalists to cover Test cricket outside India. He later worked with ESPN Star Sports as their South Asia correspondent for the iconic show *SportsCenter*; as executive producer with News X; and as senior multimedia producer with the BBC. Then, he taught Development Journalism students at the IIMC, and at Amity University as assistant professor till March 2019. He has presented papers and talks at University Center Chicago, and in Singapore, UK and Nepal. He is a guest lecturer at the IIMC, Delhi University and MICA, among others.

VIRAT
The Making of a Champion

**NEERAJ JHA &
VIDHANSHU KUMAR**

First published in 2019 by Hachette India
(Registered name: Hachette Book Publishing India Pvt. Ltd)
An Hachette UK company
www.hachetteindia.com

1

ISBN 978-93-88322-25-6

Hachette Book Publishing India Pvt. Ltd
4th & 5th Floors, Corporate Centre
Plot No. 94, Sector 44, Gurugram - 122003, India

Typeset by
by Manmohan Kumar, Delhi

Printed and bound in India
by Manipal Technologies Limited, Manipal

To my parents – Bimal Nath Jha and Sunaina Jha,
for always giving me the freedom to choose in my life;
and my better half, Nilu Jha, who has always
encouraged me at all important moments of my life

Neeraj Jha

To my father Chandra Mohan Sinha and mother
Shobha Sinha;
my uncle, Late B.K. Sinha, who ignited the passion
for sports in me;
All Bhawani Bhawan family members; and
above all, my grandfather – Late Nageshwar Prasad,
who continues to inspire us

Vidhanshu Kumar

Virat before the Tri-Series in the West Indies in 2013

Contents

1

The boy who wanted to play

It all began in the summer of 1998.

On 30 May, a particularly hot day, a Delhi-based lawyer, Prem Kohli, ferried his two children, Vikas and Virat – both staunch Sachin fans – to a cricket camp in west Delhi.

A heat wave was sweeping across the entire subcontinent, the thermometer was touching the mid-40s, and prayers for rain were on everyone's lips. Like the weather, the political temperature in India, and beyond too, was hitting an all-time high. Under Prime Minister Atal Bihari Vajpayee, the nation had tested nuclear bombs in Pokhran in Rajasthan, and Pakistan had threatened to do the same (and it did so on the day Virat's father first took him to the cricket camp).

This event sparked off a series of economic restrictions laid down against both nuclear-testing nations, India and Pakistan, by the USA and other countries, and put a strain on the Indian economy. In Delhi and other cities, the price of essential commodities skyrocketed. But this was also a time of hope.

The Indian middle class was rising, determined to stay afloat above a million challenges, to fulfil their dreams of a liberalized, globalized, winning India. They worked hard to realize their ambitions and dreams – and who was a better symbol of this bright-eyed, hard-working India than a cricket genius called Sachin Ramesh Tendulkar! The Master Blaster was at the peak of his prowess in 1998, pummelling the likes of the impressive Australian bowler Damien Fleming and the other great Aussie leg-spinner Shane Warne into the stands of dust-blown Sharjah.

It was as if Sachin Tendulkar was the answer to all of India's problems and sorrows, and he was inspiring an entire generation to follow cricket like never before. It was because of Sachin that cricket camps mushroomed across the country. One such training centre, the West Delhi Cricket Academy, was run by coach Rajkumar Sharma and he was witnessing a good turnout of young hopefuls on that hot summer day.

Not just fun and games

Among the 250-odd kids who had lined up to register, one young boy caught the coach's attention. 'I remember noticing this pretty chubby, pretty naughty sort of youngster, who was not even ten, registering enthusiastically,' the coach recalls. 'He had come with his father and brother.' It was the younger sibling who was the promising powerhouse.

Still, at his age, mop-haired Virat was among the younger members in the camp and it was certainly not going to be easy for him.

The boy was there to be a batsman, which meant that his days of playing cricket with soft balls in lanes and backyards were over. A cricket ball is made of cork and is covered with a leather case sewn together with somewhat raised seams. At 160 grams, when thrown from a distance of 22 yards (20.12 m) at a speed of 100 kmph or more (the typical speed of a fast car on the highway, or a cheetah!), this ball can hurt badly, if it hits any part of the body. Coach Sharma had a difficult task at hand – to make a proper, balanced batsman out of an enthusiastic gully cricketer.

Virat had to grow up quickly and grow strong. He had to face bowlers who were quite a few years older – and much taller! – but that didn't seem to bother him. There was an unshakable self-assurance about him, much beyond his years, that baffled even a seasoned coach like Sharma. 'After only a month or so I could make out that he was the best in his age group,' Coach Sharma says. 'As a player, he looked so good for his age. What stood out was that he was not afraid of anyone and was willing to play the seniors from day one. He was confident and had tremendous self-belief.'

It is said that cricket is a game played 'between the ears'; it is a game where mental strength is a huge factor in the magic mix for victory, and Coach Sharma believed that young Virat was very sure of himself. What Virat needed was someone to help him sharpen the technical aspects of his game.

This was easier said than done.

Wrongs and rights

As a young, right-handed batsman, Virat knew his own mind. He was developing his own unique style in gathering runs. With a strong bottom-handed grip, Virat was mainly an onside player.

The flick off his pads was fast becoming Virat's mainstay shot. Even when playing offside cover drives, Virat would still trust his bottom hand, which was something that even the best players wouldn't do. That's because when one plays with a strong bottom hand, there is a risk of scooping the ball in the air and offering the chance of a catch to the opposition. But Virat was defying all such rules and playing cover drives successfully.

Initially, everything seemed rosy as Virat evolved his own ingenious, if not technically perfect, ways of getting runs. However, in cricket it's easy to slip up due to a lack of technique. Good bowlers are clever at sussing the batsman out – they quickly weigh up his strengths and weaknesses, and then change their bowling plan into a strategy that exposes the batsman's shortcomings.

Soon, Virat was facing the same situation. Bowlers were beginning to call him out on his flick shots. So, when he was out leg before wicket (lbw) for the umpteenth time while playing the flick shot from around the middle stump, despite being cautioned against it many times before, Coach Sharma was furious.

'It was for playing the flick shot that I scolded him the most,' Coach Sharma recalls. 'This was because he used to play the flick early in his innings without pulling his leg towards the leg stump.' Coaches won't stop a young batsman from playing a flick shot off the pads, but they are usually not happy when the same flick is played from the middle or off stumps as it carries a risk of taking an edge and getting caught behind the wicket.

Sharma set a regimen for Virat in which he had to resist playing the flick from around his middle stump. Virat too had realized his mistake and was determined not to repeat it and endanger his time at the crease. Day in and day out, month after month, Virat practised until he was able to iron out this weakness.

'He was getting out lbw a lot in the early days, but he mastered that shot,' Coach Sharma recounts. 'He worked really hard on it. Earlier, he was not going forward full length to approach the ball, but slowly that was changing too.'

And soon, a polished player, with fine-tuned shots, began to emerge.

Virat still loved to flick, but he had learnt to be patient, to wait for the right ball. While his naturally strong bottom hand remained, Virat made sure that he was in the correct position to play the shot. With these errors corrected, he soon became unbeatable in his small circle. Virat was already doing things right.

The boy would never miss a practice session. He listened to his coaches and worked hard to amend his mistakes. So much so that in the tournament that he played under Coach Sharma in 2003, five years after he had joined the camp, Virat was simply invincible.

'The Delhi Development Authority's Sports Complex ground in Hari Nagar [where the tournament was being played] is not very large,' says Coach Sharma, 'but it can still challenge young players. Virat was clearing the ropes regularly with – fours or sixes – and also hitting delectable shots in all directions. It was a sheer delight to watch. I was so happy that Virat had put right his mistake and was ready to take on any challenge.'

Indeed, he was. In that tournament of six games – which included three league games and a quarter-final, a semi-final and the final – Virat was out only once! Of course, he was also the highest scorer, playing beautiful shots all around the ground. This was a big personal victory for Virat. He had made his first tracks towards perfection. With hard work and discipline, he had turned his weaknesses into strengths – the sign of a future champion.

'Smell the leather' – that's what the coaching manual says about playing a forward-defensive block – stretch out your front foot, meet the ball under the eye, so close that you could actually sniff it. This shot was a winning

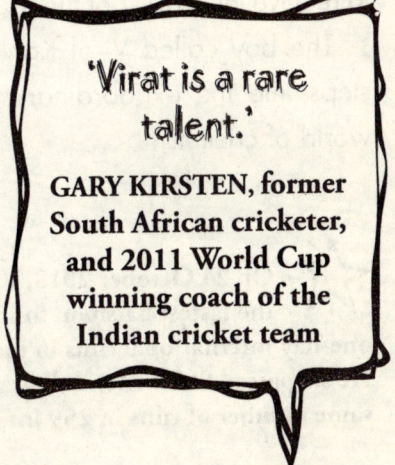

'Virat is a rare talent.'

GARY KIRSTEN, former South African cricketer, and 2011 World Cup winning coach of the Indian cricket team

one in the arsenal of cricket legends like Sunil Gavaskar and Mohinder Amarnath, but when a fourteen-year-old displayed skills way beyond his age while playing this stroke, he was sure to catch the attention of the people watching closely. And it was not only the defensive blocks, but also the many shots he played around the park that day, which made everyone sit up and notice this talent.

Even though this was just a school-level tournament, there was a definite buzz going around about it. Most eyes – those of the players and the odd spectators gathered around – were riveted on the guest of honour, Indian strike bowler Ashish Nehra, who had just returned from his heroic performance in the 2003 ICC World Cup in South Africa. However, Nehra himself could not take his eyes off the young bundle of talent who was flooring everyone with his batting prowess that day and was soon to receive the 'Player of the Tournament' award from him.

The boy called Virat Kohli was taking his first few steps into the extraordinary, and often exasperating, world of cricket.

On 24 October 2018, Virat became the fastest batsman to score 10,000 one-day international runs in just 205 innings. He surpassed Sachin Tendulkar's record for the same number of runs in 259 innings.

Virat after India's win against South Africa at the
Moses Mabhida Stadium, Durban, in 2011

2

The boy who wanted to become better and better

In the cricket-crazy country called India, there is hardly a home without a bat and a ball. Into just such a home, Virat was born to Saroj and Prem Kohli on 5 November 1988. Indeed, these were the 'toys' that Virat picked up when he was just three. He would often ask his father to throw the ball at him, which he swung as hard as he could.

His mother took care of the household and the family of five that included Virat's older siblings: his brother Vikas – seven years older, and sister Bhavna – nine years older. Virat's father practised law and also dabbled in small businesses. They lived in a modest house in west Delhi, where it was easy to get lost in the twisty lanes of the densely populated colonies.

Virat studied at the local Vishal Bharti Public School until class IX and then moved to Saviour Convent. At Vishal Bharti, he played cricket whenever he got the chance. After school, it became his favourite pastime and he would scamper off to play gully cricket with the neighbouring boys as soon as he got home.

Prem Kohli noticed young Virat's unusual keenness for the game. Perhaps he saw the glimmer of something special in his son and decided that he needed to help him hone his skills. That was when he took Virat to Coach Raj Kumar Sharma's cricket academy. Though Virat also trained briefly with two other academies in his early years of cricket, it was Coach Sharma under whom he shaped his game.

On Virat's first day at the academy, Prem Kohli told Coach Sharma that he was to be a surrogate parent and a mentor for young Virat. He was putting his son in good hands, the best available to him. Coach Sharma, in turn, remembers Virat during his early days of training as a talented young boy who was playful too. It was difficult to keep him quiet – he would either be training hard, or be up to some harmless mischief.

Virat proved to be a good student of the game. Coach Sharma's academy was around 5 km from his home, and when he was old enough, Virat would speedily cycle the distance with his kitbag perched on the bike's handlebars. Coach Sharma says that even now when Virat is batting for India, he can catch glimpses of the enthusiastic boy that he was when he first stepped into cricket.

Being the youngest of the three children, Virat was showered with a lot of affection by his parents. He was very close to his father, who would accompany his youngest child to the coaching academy as often as possible, driving him to the practice session on his Kinetic Honda scooter, or watching him closely from the sidelines. As Virat worked hard on his game, through sun and rain, never missing a day's session, the proud father could sense that a dream – that of his son becoming a professional cricket player for India – was turning into a reality.

Along with his obvious passion for the game, Virat was also discovering his father's role as the guiding light in his quest of learning the game. Prem Kohli was Virat's biggest support, instilling in him the right values to make a good sportsman. As Virat wrote on his Father's Day post on Twitter on 17 June 2018, his father taught him about having faith in his own hard work, not looking for favours for anything, and believing in his own abilities to reach the greatest heights.[1] These simple, golden guidelines became the founding principles of Virat's life, and later, the core of his professional life.

Prem Kohli's hopes gradually began to take shape as Virat began to excel at the junior level. As a result of his tough training regimen, Virat was slowly growing into a master batsman of his age group. Even though he was playing with cricketers much older than him, Virat was unafraid and bold, and his attitude – for which he was to be in headlines later – was beginning to show. A natural and instinctive player of the game, Virat was ready to bat at any spot in the batting order and was turning out to be a great team person. Even during the training sessions, it was impossible to stop Virat. He would go on, over after over, until the coach had to literally force him to end practice.

Under-15 upwards

After five years with Coach Sharma, Virat began to make his mark in the Under-15 (U-15) and Under-17 (U-17) age-group levels. He was fast becoming the highest scorer for Delhi in the age-group tournaments and this was already garnering him accolades.

In 2002, Virat played for the Delhi team in the U-15 tournament and scored a double hundred, demonstrating his knack for scoring big runs even at the age of fourteen. In the Polly Umrigar Trophy during 2002–03, his batting ability was on full display as he became the highest scorer in the tournament with his aggregate of 172 runs per innings at an average of 34.40. Following his consistently superior performances, he was made the captain of the U-15 Delhi side for the same tournament next year.

Responsibility seemed to instill in him an even deeper hunger for runs. In 2003 and 2004, Virat plundered the opposition's bowling to become the leading run scorer once again, this time with 390 runs in just 5 innings and a superlative average of 78 runs per innings.

With strong performances at the U-15 level under his belt, it was but natural for Virat to progress to the U-17 level. In 2004, Virat was called up to join Delhi's U-17 team for the Vijay Merchant Trophy – named after the legendary batsman and bowler who is widely regarded as the founder of the 'Bombay school of batting', which emphasized perfect technique. Virat was soon to leave an indelible mark on the tournament.

Competition in the Vijay Merchant Trophy matches is quite stiff as players from across the country take part in it. However, in only four matches, Virat scored 470 runs at a Don-Bradman-like average of 117.50. During the course of the tournament, he scored two centuries that included a chanceless 251 not out (that means he played without offering any opportunity to be dismissed) against Himachal Pradesh! His remarkable run rate continued as he became the top scorer once again, with 757 runs in seven matches. This time his average was an incredible 84.11 again!

Virat's aggregates, year after year, were becoming difficult to ignore and Delhi's senior selectors started to take note of this talented young star. What also worked in Virat's favour was the fact that he was not making a parachute landing in the Delhi team. His rise to the top was a gradual, well-earned one – step by step, run by run – as he laboured hard to make himself a better cricketer every day. His sweat and strife were about to bear result.

In February 2006, Virat was selected to play in a List A match against the Services (the Services Cricket Association represents the Indian Armed Forces). Although Virat made this debut at the senior level, he did not get to bat in that match. His first major international breakthrough came in July, when he was picked for the India Under-19 (U-19) team to play against England.

Batting conditions are very different in England when compared to India. Many fabled Indian batting maestros have struggled in English conditions. There is

'He is just an unbelievable batsman. No need to say more.'

BRIAN LARA, former West Indian international cricketer

a lot more swing and bounce on pitches there. So batsmen from the Indian subcontinent, who are not used to such conditions, need to play with supreme control and make sure they don't edge the ball to the wicketkeeper or the slips and get caught. The in-swinging balls, if not played properly, also run the risk of knocking off the stumps.

No doubt the conditions were challenging, but Virat's belief in himself and his die-hard attitude came in good stead as he notched up an awesome average of 105 runs in the tournament's one-day series. In the Test series of three matches, Virat once again showed his class with a good average of 49 runs. India managed to win both the one-day and Test series, and the team's then coach, Lalchand Rajput, commented that Virat's strong technique, both against spin and fast bowling, impressed everyone. He was the one to watch in the future.

Virat's excellent run with the India U-19 team continued when the Indian team toured arch-rivals Pakistan in September the same year. In the Test series there, Virat's average was a very respectable 58, while he had an average of 41.66 per innings in the limited-overs matches.

This shining string of high scores in the domestic age-group tournaments followed by a first-rate run in the overseas venues of England and Pakistan made Delhi selectors look closely at Virat once again. The probability of a promotion was high.

Right for Ranji

The elevation due to Virat came in November 2006 when he got called up to the prestigious Delhi's side in the Ranji Trophy. This is a domestic first-class cricket championship, named after Ranjitsinhji, the first Indian cricketer to play international cricket. The Ranji Trophy is played between teams representing regional and state cricket associations in India. Currently, there are thirty-seven teams, with all twenty-nine states and two Union Territories featuring at least one representation.

This was how Virat made his debut against Tamil Nadu that season. Batting at number five in the order, Virat was dismissed for just 10 runs. However, his attitude and work ethic were well recognized in the star-studded Delhi squad, which included Gautam Gambhir, Aakash Chopra, Shikhar Dhawan, Ashish Nehra and Virender Sehwag.

It was while he was playing for the Delhi Ranji team that Virat acquired his nickname, Cheeku. Coach Sharma tells the story: 'One day Virat came for practice with a new haircut. Someone in the dressing room said that he looked like Cheeku the rabbit from the popular children's magazine, *Champak* [published by the Delhi Press Group since 1969 in India]. And the name stuck!'

Ashish Nehra, India's former left-arm fast bowler, recalls the grit and determination that defined Virat even at that early age: 'In the 2006–07 season, when he [Virat] was selected for the Delhi Ranji side, I was part of the same team. Bowling to him in the nets, I realized what great timing Virat had in hitting the ball – he always found that extra second to execute a shot.'

It wasn't Virat's innate talent alone that impressed Nehra, nor merely the perfect clocking of Virat's stroke play. 'What I liked the most was his resolve to always do well,' says Nehra. 'Whether it was his batting, or fielding, or training, he always came to it with the utmost intensity and determination. Not only that, he also enjoyed those moments! When you start to enjoy what you do, you are bound to succeed, and that's what Virat started practising very early.'

Sharp-eyed Nehra also identifies one more secret of Virat's success. 'Usually when someone is trying to make their mark, they work very hard,' Nehra explains. 'After a few years of success, we see a plateau, even a downslide, in the effort they put in. However, it was – and is – the very opposite with Virat. Once he achieved a milestone, his intensity and workouts increased. He has constantly been raising the bar.'

The boy who wanted to get better and better was justifying the faith his coaches and his father put in him. Especially his father. Virat always felt that his life was influenced by his dad and that his own sense of 'judgement' was something he learned from his father. Prem Kohli had led a life full of struggle and had sacrificed many of his personal needs and wants for his family. His son was now mirroring his sense of purpose in achieving what he had set out to do. Virat once said in an interview with *LiveMint* (livemint.com)[2] that his stubbornness came from his father, from the unwavering pursuit of a self-made man, a value drilled deep in young Virat.

As the strong-willed teenager enjoyed his triumphs in the India U-19 side and his subsequent call to the Ranji Delhi side, Virat was also a little worried because Prem Kohli was not keeping too well...

Virat holds the record for scoring the fastest ODI century by an Indian. He achieved the feat in just 52 balls against Australia in 2013 in Jaipur, Rajasthan.

3

The boy who cried twice... in one day

Former England captain and cricket philosopher Mike Brearley once said that genius is a combination of the 'instinctual' with 'passionate devotion and hard work'.[3] And Virat was proving that this was true in his case as he made his mark in age-group cricket (cricket in bands of age groups, such as Under-15s, 17s and 19s).

His coaches, rivals and peers were already in admiration of Virat's love for the game, his never-say-die attitude and his passion on the field, which was generously mixed with open aggression. After the conclusion of the India U-19 squad's tour of England – where Virat showed some classy batting – the team coach and former India player, Lalchand Rajput, said, 'Kohli showed strong technical skills against both pace and spin.'[4]

But then, cricket is a game that tests a player's mental strength repeatedly, and in unforeseen situations. The year 2006 was one of the most important years of Virat's life – both personally and professionally. Just as Virat was making a stellar mark on age-group cricket in the country, he was soon going to face the greatest test of his life. And it all happened during the Ranji Trophy.

DAY 1: 17 DECEMBER 2006

Virat was selected for the playing XI against Karnataka in the Ranji Trophy Group 'A' match at Delhi's iconic Feroz Shah Kotla Ground. This day belonged to the opposition as they scored 299 runs at the loss of only 3 wickets.

DAY 2: 18 DECEMBER 2006

The Delhi Ranji team lost 5 wickets chasing Karnataka's mammoth first innings total of 446 runs. With half the side back in the pavilion, it was an uphill task for Virat and the rest of the team to save the match.

Virat walked out along with wicketkeeper Puneet Bisht, and they both helped Delhi reach a score of 103 runs at the end of the day's play, without losing any more wickets. Virat held his ground and ended the day unbeaten at 40 runs. These two were the last recognized batsmen in the team and this partnership was vital as they were facing a follow-on the next day. Virat had gone home and slept early as he was tired after the day's game; he also had to go on the pitch early the next day.

DAY 3: 19 DECEMBER 2006

This was a crucial, life-changing day for Virat.

Very late on 18 December, Prem Kohli suffered a heart attack. His family had tried to get help from the neighbours, to check if there was any doctor close-by, but since it was so late at night, no one responded. By the time the ambulance arrived, around 2.30 a.m., it was all over. Fifty-four-year-old Prem Kohli was gone.

In the morning, when Virat found out that his father had passed away, he began to cry. He was all set to go and bat to save the match, and now he looked at a terrible choice – whether to cremate his father, or to complete his innings for Delhi.

When Virat called Coach Sharma in the morning and told him what had happened, the latter was in shock. 'I still remember,' recounts the coach, 'he called me, crying, saying, "My father is no more". I was shaken too, because his father had become a dear friend of mine. Virat asked me, "What should I do?" I consoled him and told him to wait, telling him I would call him back in ten minutes.

'When I called back, I asked him, "What do *you* want to do?" and he said, "I want to go and play." So I encouraged him to play. I said, "The team needs you and this is the time to show your character". And he did. For him, not completing a cricket match was a sin.'

The news of his father's death had already travelled to the Delhi team's dressing room. The next batsman in the order – Chetanya Nanda – was informed that he should pad up.

However, to the disbelief of his teammates, and everyone else there, Virat arrived at the dot. At 7.30 a.m., at the start of the third day, he declared he was ready to play.

Former India paceman Ashish Nehra, who was a key senior member of the Delhi team, says he was surprised when he saw that Virat had come to join the team that day. 'But it only shows his strong character and how seriously he thinks about his team and game,' Nehra says now. 'It was a sad time and as a senior member I could only console him, but he showed us way back then the glimpse of what he is today.'

The team needed him desperately, but they also told him that he was needed more at home. However, Virat insisted that he wanted to bat.

The then Delhi Ranji team captain Mithun Manhas was amazed to see the youngster's determination. He said in an interview with *The Telegraph* (*India*) after the match: 'We asked him what made him come here. And we also told him that if he decided to go back and be with his family, the entire team would support him. He decided to play. That is an act of great commitment to the team and his innings turned out to be crucial.'[5]

The most surprising part was yet to come.

To the astonishment of his teammates and the opposition, Virat saved Delhi from the follow-on. That morning, along with Puneet Bisht who scored 156, Virat saw his side through safely with an amazing spate of runs. He played for 281 minutes and faced 238 balls before he was out at 90 just before lunch, given caught behind off a ball by Balachandran Akhil, Karnataka's spearhead, who took 5 wickets in that innings. The replays, however, showed that the bat had brushed the pad and not touched the bat at all. Those were the days when the Third Umpire (or TV Umpire), an off-field umpire who makes the final decision with the help of replays and other technology in cases referred to him by the two on-field umpires, had not been introduced yet at the domestic level in all matches.

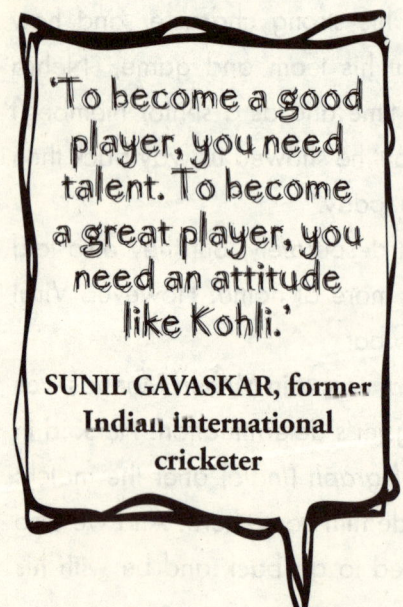

'To become a good player, you need talent. To become a great player, you need an attitude like Kohli.'

SUNIL GAVASKAR, former Indian international cricketer

At around noon, Virat watched the replay of his dismissal in the dressing room. He was not happy with the umpire's decision and frustration was written all over his face.

Coach Sharma recalls that he called Virat after two and a half hours. Virat was crying again, but this time it was not for this father. 'He told me that the on-field umpire had declared him out wrongly,' Sharma remembers. 'I told him whatever has happened has happened – and he should leave for his father's funeral. It was the day his father had died, and there he was crying about the umpire's incorrect decision – that showed how cricket meant everything to him.'

Virat's father – his closest friend, guide and mentor – was cremated later that evening.

Former India Test opener and the then Delhi coach Chetan Chauhan was amazed at Virat's dedication. 'We left the decision to him,' Chauhan recalls now. 'We were all amazed to see him getting ready to bat. That was just a glimpse of Virat Kohli as a great cricketer in the making. His decision showed how mentally strong he is. He was determined to take the team to safety. Hats off to his attitude and determination! These are the signs of a great player. At the time, I saw a superstar in the making.'

'It was very tough for a young kid whose father's body was lying at home, to go and play a cricket match,'

Coach Sharma adds. 'That shows how committed he was to cricket and his team. Virat matured very early because of his father's death. I was always there for him, but he started taking responsibility for himself and acting maturely from that time onwards.'

Virat knew that his father was gone, and then more than ever, he wanted to fulfil his dad's dreams. He knew his team needed him and that the match could be saved. In many interviews, Virat later said that this was the moment when he had made up his mind to make cricket his career. It was on that day he decided that he was going to play for his country. His father played a huge role in Virat becoming a cricketer, and, in turn, the sport became a sort of 'madness' for him. He never once thought of the possibility that it might not happen. He never once thought – 'what if it doesn't work out?'.

That day, Virat's mindset about the game changed forever. All he could think of was that he had to play for his country and live that dream for his father.

An impossible decision

Putting aside his personal tragedy to pull his team from the jaws of defeat revealed Virat's mental strength and his love for the game. For him, it seemed, life was cricket and it stood above everything else. There could not have been a bigger, better example of how a teenager learned to handle responsibility from an early age. He had lost his father so young, the family business was not doing too well, they were staying in a rented house... these were tough times for Virat and his family. But he transformed from an eighteen-year-old into a mature adult overnight.

His mother Saroj noted that Virat changed after that day. He started taking every match seriously, and hated not being selected for the playing XI and sitting on the bench. From then on, it seemed as if his life hinged totally on cricket.[6]

It was the moment that changed Virat as a person. The night his father passed away was possibly the hardest time in his life, but the call to play the morning after, Virat has said in interviews, came instinctively to him. In one such interview with CNN, he said, 'That's where, maybe, I got the confidence people speak about.'[7]

From then to now, Virat's single-minded focus on the field and his driven aggression – both hallmarks of his game – have been unshakable. His passion, hard work and 100 per cent commitment to the game have already earned him a special place among cricketing greats.

Many players go through phases of unbearable struggle, but what makes one different from the others is the way he or she handles the situation. Virat has been the perfect example of how to deal with a crisis. The other stellar instance is of Virat's long-time idol, Sachin Tendulkar, who, during the 1999 World Cup, lost his father in the middle of the tournament in England. It was the biggest blow to his life, yet Sachin went to India for the funeral and then returned to join his team – he then scored a century and led India to an important victory against Kenya. But Sachin was much older than Virat had been in a similar situation.

Virat's story of that fateful day in December 2006 has been forever imprinted in Feroz Shah Kotla Ground's history. It is the real-life tale of a boy who loved cricket more than anything else – and it wouldn't be long before cricket would, as they say, love him back just as much.

Virat became the fastest to score 1,000 ODI runs in a calendar year, making them in 2018 in 11 innings. He beat Hashim Amla's record of 15 innings to score those many runs in 2010.

Virat plays a pull shot

4

The boy who moved ahead real quick

An eye-witness to Virat's dynamic performances on the pitch was his U-19 team captain, teammate and brilliant run scorer from Kanpur, Tanmay Srivastava.

'Jai *to woh hee hai ji*, the real superstar, I am Veeru of the *jodi* (He is Jai, the real superstar, I am Veeru of the pair)' says Srivastava now, with a broad grin. There is a context to this comparison. Just like Amitabh Bachchan (Jai) and Dharmendra (Veeru) worked as a pair to rid a village from the terror of Gabbar Singh in the iconic 1970s movie *Sholay*, Virat Kohli and Tanmay Srivastava formed many winning partnerships to pull Indian batting out of the deep hole it would often find itself in.

So often would they find themselves in rescue operations on the field – and successfully accomplish them – that the cricketing fraternity came to know them as the 'Jai' and 'Veeru' of Indian cricket.

One such series was in England in the summer of 2006, which consisted of three ODIs and three Tests. The U-19 team was led by Srivastava, who played a captain's knock of 182 runs in the final Test. Virat and he were among the top scorers.

Following that came the U-19 team's tour of Pakistan. There are very few rivalries in sport that can be compared to the India–Pakistan one on the cricket field. While the competition between the senior teams is well documented, the intensity has percolated down to age-group matches as well. The India U-19 cricket team too had a history of passionate encounters with their Pakistani counterparts.

Just a few months before the contest, on 19 February of the same year, winter was melting away in the oceanic breezes of Colombo when the Indian colts had taken on defending champions Pakistan in the final of the 2006 U-19 World Cup. The Pakistan team was represented by the likes of Sarfaraz Ahmed, Imad Wasim, Anwar Ali and Nasir Jamshed, all of whom went on to play for the senior national side later. The Indian XI were no less accomplished, with Rohit Sharma, Ravindra Jadeja, Cheteshwar Pujara, Manish Pandey and Piyush Chawla in the line-up.

As the one-day 50-over match progressed, the Indian bowlers did well to restrict Pakistan to 109 runs and it looked like India would dethrone Pakistan to win the Cup. However, as they often can, Pakistan came up with an unpredictable show in their bowling. Soon their seamers had reduced India to 6 wickets for just 9 runs! India eventually lost the match by 38 runs and Pakistan became the U-19 world champions for the second time in succession.

This was an important victory for Pakistan, something they would not hesitate to throw in India's face when the India U-19 team visited them for the two-match bilateral Test series that year. *'Inhe* Colombo *ki tarah jaldi wapas* pavilion *bhej do, jaldi-jaldi* (Make them walk back to the pavilion just like in Colombo),' was the chatter from behind the stumps as the Indians took the crease. Srivastava recalls how the Pakistani side, buoyed by a boisterous home crowd, was busy engaging the Indians in 'small chats'. (The terms 'chat' is interchangeable with 'sledging' by which some players try to gain a psychological advantage by insulting or verbally intimidating the opponents.)

In those days, Cheteshwar Pujara would open the innings while Virat and Srivastava would typically bat at number four and number five. Sadly, India got off to a bad start in the first Test in Rawalpindi, losing 2 early wickets. However, Virat and Srivastava both hit crucial 50s and India posted a respectable 289 in the first innings. Following this, Pakistan fell short by 142 runs in their first innings and never recovered, as India pressed on for a major victory.

The teams moved to Peshawar for the second and last Test match of the series. The Pakistan team was desperate to level the series and the 'chatter' grew even louder. As luck would have it, the Indian team once again lost early wickets, leaving Virat and Srivastava to carry out a challenging rescue job.

'Every now and then, the slips fielders or the keeper would remind us about the big defeat in the U-19 World Cup,' Srivastava recalls. It is difficult for the batsman on strike to concentrate on batting when four or five players surround the batsman and talk continuously, trying to erode his morale and destroy his concentration.

'Virat was beginning to find his groove and was at least half as aggressive then compared to what he later became,' says Srivastava. 'We had a chat during the partnership, and decided to keep calm, concentrate on the deliveries and let the bat do the talking.' It was turning out to be a great batting partnership in which they complemented each other.

One of the most beautiful sights in the game of cricket is a left-handed batsman hitting perfectly timed cover drives that pierce an offside heavily packed with fielders. One such batsman was Indian cricketer Sourav Ganguly, who was called 'the god of the offside', so graceful were his cover drives. Srivastava too was developing as a fine lefty and his favourite shots were elegant cover drives that blazed across the carpet. Virat also had a penchant for cover drives, along with his patent flick shots.

Faced with hostile Pakistani bowling, these two young batsmen counter-attacked with precision and style, and began to tire the Pakistani bowlers. The duo had added 180 runs for the third wicket, when Virat was out after a well-made 83. Srivastava stuck to the crease to raise a mammoth double century, before being dismissed for a whopping 220. The Indian team declared at 611 for the loss of 9 wickets.

This was too high a score for Pakistan to chase. Both their innings folded modestly, and India registered a resounding win by an innings and 240 runs. Following this victory, the selectors started to notice remarkable performers such as Srivastava, Ishant Sharma, Piyush Chawla and, of course, Virat.

Never say die

In their junior years, both Virat and Tanmay Srivastava had been scoring big. In fact, Srivastava would outscore

Virat on many occasions, but Virat's mental strength was quickly becoming his winning asset and setting him apart from the others. So, when the selectors sat down to decide the skipper for the 2008 U-19 World Cup, Virat pipped others to the post.

One of the selectors, Rakesh Parikh, later told the Indian press that it was a tough choice between Srivastava – who had captained India for three series, and Virat – who showed leadership abilities but was untested in the captaincy department. Finally, Virat was selected because the selectors saw match-winning qualities in him. He disliked defeat and his batting displayed his desire to win. He liked to dominate the game, something that has not changed to date. So intense is his wish to win that once, during a U-19 league game, when Indian bowlers were not able to get a breakthrough, Virat himself decided to bowl!

It was this attitude of never conceding defeat that the selectors favoured. This was a new pedestal for Virat, a sign that not only his technical prowess but his leadership skills too were being recognized. Another reason for Virat's promotion was his strong run in the domestic games. In the five first-class matches of that season, Virat scored 373 runs at an average of 53, a brilliant set of figures.

Among the runs

Virat led the U-19 team to the World Cup held in Malaysia from 17 February to 2 March 2008. India, placed in Group B of the tournament, defeated Papua New Guinea, South Africa and the West Indies. While Tanmay Srivastava scored a classy 83 against Papua New Guinea, Virat came up with a superlative 106 against the Caribbean side in the last group-stage match.

Then India went on to beat England in the quarter-final and defeated a confident New Zealand team in the semi-final, where Virat displayed yet another facet of his robust character. Despite losing early wickets, the Kiwis were consolidating and beginning to build a strong total. The bowlers were failing to find their line length and mark. To the surprise of the opposition, and of even his own team, Virat turned to bowl himself. He clean bowled a well settled Fraser Colson for 32 and then got the scalp of Ross Greg Morgan as well, who was declared out lbw for just 1 run.

So competitive was Virat that he took up bowling when he felt his team needed the push, even though he was not a regular bowler himself. Still, he was not just filling in for other bowlers; no, he was bowling to take wickets – and he captured two crucial ones.

The final was played against South Africa. Even though India had defeated the Proteas team in a league match before this one, this was a different game – a World Cup final, which could make or break careers.

India batted first and once again lost the openers cheaply. Srivastava, coming at one down, stitched a patient 46 in 74 balls. Virat also sought to hit top form. Unfortunately, he was dismissed for only 19, but not before the two had added 47 runs for the fourth wicket. Led by Wayne Parnell, an aggressive bowling attack from the South Africans resulted in the Indian team getting bowled out for a paltry 159 runs.

This was a modest target to defend, but Virat spoke with his team members during the break, motivating them to give their best. Even though the target was low, the opposition had to get one *more* run than that, and the bowlers and fielders were pepped up to not concede the smallest inch.

South Africa lost 3 quick wickets for 11

> 'Virat Kohli's success does not surprise you. His failures do.'
>
> **SANJAY MANJREKAR, former Indian international cricketer**

runs, and things looked good for India, when suddenly rain stopped play. A revised target of 116 runs in 25 overs was set under the Duckworth–Lewis method. (This is a mathematical formulation worked out to calculate the target score for the team batting second in a limited-overs cricket match that is interrupted by weather or other circumstances.) Virat was charged up and his electric passion was transmitted to his teammates, sparking off a spirited display of skill and strength. India restricted South Africa to 103 runs for 8 wickets in 25 overs, and won the U-19 World Cup for the second time since 2000.

This was another life-changing moment for Virat, and this time it was a turning point in his career. Many of the young members of that team went on to play for India, but it was only Virat who garnered the greatest achievements because of his hunger and dedication.

In fact, it's interesting to examine how two equally talented and hard-working cricketers of the same age charted completely different career graphs. Both Tanmay Srivastava and Virat Kohli were high scorers, both captained India at the U-19 level, and both were touted as the chosen ones for the future. So why did their lives play out differently?

While Virat's career launched steeply, many other players from the Word-Cup-winning U-19 side, including

Srivastava, were not as fortunate. 'The key is consistency,' Srivastava himself says. 'While it is good to score big runs in big matches, one has to make every innings count. I feel I made fewer runs, I should have scored more. Usually when players score heavily at the U-19 level, they are noticed by the selectors. It becomes important to hit consistently to be taken seriously by them.'

Srivastava also points out another feather in Virat's cap – his ability as a 'finisher'. 'He kept hitting big runs,' says Srivastava, 'but his most impressive quality was the ability to finish games, something that I admire.'

Former Australian captain Michael Clarke, who saw Virat during the U-19 days, says that Virat's competitive nature would always make him stand out. Coach Sharma mentions another vital factor in Virat's arsenal – his will to keep on improving in every aspect of the game. Usually when a player is established, he or she often gets complacent and works only to maintain his or her position. But Virat was different. He always wanted to get better and better.

'He never rested on his laurels,' says Coach Sharma. 'Even while on tour, Virat would regularly call me and we had long discussions – on how to improve little technical aspects of batting, on mental fortitude, and more. Virat is never satisfied with an achievement and always wants to do even better.'

It was this trait – to constantly enhance himself – that made Virat scale greater heights. He was not competing against fellow players, he was competing with himself! With his mindset and his excellent work code, no one doubted that Virat would one day become a great player.

Meanwhile, Virat became a Delhi Ranji team regular and it was only be a matter of time before he would be knocking on the doors of the Indian national squad.

Chasing a score brings out the best in Virat. He has scored 25 centuries while chasing – the highest by any batsman in the world. He has done this in just 102 innings, compared to Sachin Tendulkar's 17 centuries in 232 innings.

5

The boy who made it to the India XI

Virat was shaping up excellently as a cricketer. But he was one among many. In a country where cricket is an obsession, it isn't easy to stand out among hundreds and thousands of talented young cricketers and make it to the top.

With around 400 million people in the ten- to twenty-four-year age bracket, India has the world's largest youth population. The game of cricket, with its generous funding by sponsors and advertisers, and the spotlight of fame and fortune that follows its shiniest stars, is on the wish list of many young cricketers and their families. Cricket academies are brimming with young players nursing dreams of making it to a team, whether domestic, national, or the one for the Indian Premier League (IPL).

There was only one make-or-break test, and that was if Virat could make it to the national squad and compete at the international level. To play for India, you had to be someone extra special.

Virat's journey from an aggressive U-19 player to his debut at the international level was, by now, folklore. Cricket fans had had a good glimpse of his aggressive celebration style in the 2008 U-19 World Cup in Malaysia – holding the victory wicket stump in one hand, and fist-pumping the air with the other! As a strong player who led his team from the front, Virat had won many hearts and much applause.

His U-19 team coach, Lalchand Rajput, known for his eye for spotting talent, was quick to point out that Virat would be the next big thing in Indian cricket. Rajput recalls an interesting story with Manjrekar. The coach noticed how good Virat was batting lower down the order and how he had a knack for standing tall in pressure situations. Rajput shared this with former India player and his Mumbai Ranji partner Sanjay Manjrekar. He told Manjrekar that he could see Virat as another Sachin, and that Virat was likely to be selected for the India national squad very soon. Manjrekar, not fully convinced, would nod or smile it away.

Then, in July 2007, during the Tri-nation U-19 tournament in Sri Lanka, between Sri Lanka, Bangladesh, and India, Rajput invited Manjrekar (a commentator for the Sri Lanka versus Bangladesh series between the national teams) to watch one of the matches. The sole purpose was to convince Manjrekar of Virat's capabilities. Manjrekar watched the match between India and Bangladesh, but, as luck would have it, Virat was out at only 21. Manjrekar wryly said that the boy still had a long way to go. When Rajput said that it was just an off day for Virat, Manjrekar felt that it was too early to judge him.

Rajput took this on as a challenge on behalf of his protégé and made it a habit of sending Manjrekar text messages every time Virat scored a hundred. He was more than confident of Virat's talent. At every opportunity, he told Manjrekar that not only would Virat play for India soon, but that he also had the qualities to captain Team India and the skill to surpass Sachin Tendulkar's records. That was an uncanny prediction because, as we all know, it has come true.

Virat was selected in the national squad for Sri Lanka's tour of India, but Rajput says that Manjrekar was still not convinced. It was only after Virat's performance in the 2011 World Cup that he told Rajput, 'You have got a great eye, and this guy is going to stay for long.'

The story of Virat's selection in the India national squad for Sri Lanka is quite a thriller. And its moral is: 'If you have the talent, no one and nothing can stop you.'

In the India XI

Nineteen-year-old Virat had emerged as the triumphant Indian captain of the 2008 U-19 World Cup and blossomed as a player to catch the selectors' attention for U-23 players in the India A team for the four-nation Emerging Players Trophy in July 2008. The tournament was to be played in Australia with S. Badrinath as captain.

From 2006 to 2008, Indian cricket had seen turbulent times in the Board of Control for Cricket in India (BCCI). A power struggle within the board was followed by the BCCI facing a rebel India Cricket League (ICL) propped up by media baron Subhash Chandra, which forced the Indian board to launch the Indian Premier League in 2008. During this period, iconic cricketer and former India captain Dilip Vengsarkar, known popularly as 'Colonel', the man with 116 Tests and 129 ODIs under his belt, took over from Kiran

> 'The more the pressure on Virat, the better he plays.'
>
> **HARBHAJAN SINGH,**
> **Indian off-spinner and**
> **cricketer**

More as chief selector. Vengsarkar had heard about Virat's prowess and travelled to Brisbane to watch him play.

The Colonel had a deep understanding of raw talent and his tenure gave India some of the finest cricketers. There are many stories of his wise insight into the final potential of a budding player, but one is most famous.

In 2003, as the man in charge of the BCCI Talent Research Development Wing (TRDW), Vengsarkar sent his development officer, Prakash Poddar, to Jamshedpur in Jharkhand, to watch a match. A twenty-three-year-old player called Mahendra Singh Dhoni made only 35 runs in that game, but Poddar was impressed by the way this fierce cricketer from Ranchi was hitting the balls. Poddar sent his recommendation to his boss, who marked Dhoni as a valuable talent. Finally, it culminated in the selection of Dhoni in the national squad in 2004, and the rest is cricketing history. The BCCI TRDW team led by Vengsarkar is also credited with spotting explosive and enduring players such as Suresh Raina and Irfan Pathan. After he took over the selection committee, Vengsarkar's first big decision was the appointment of Dhoni as captain of the Indian T20 team. In return, Dhoni and its team won for India her first World T20 title.

Throwing youngsters in the deep end was characteristic of Vengsarkar's tenure. Earlier that year, ace hitter Rohit Sharma and attacking all-rounder Manoj Tiwary had been picked for the tri-series in Australia. But Virat was Vengsarkar's master stroke.

The 2008 Emerging Players tournament, following a 50-over ODI format, was held between 14 and 26 July in Brisbane. The four nations participating in the tournament were India, New Zealand, Australia and South Africa. In the first few matches, Virat played in the middle order. But in the fourth match, he came out as an opener against New Zealand. Vengsarkar watched as Virat, opening for the team for the first time, dismantled the New Zealand attack and scored 120 not out. He and Shikhar Dhawan contributed a valuable 93 runs to their first-wicket partnership. The New Zealand team, with Trent Boult, Corey Anderson, Jesse Ryder and Martin Guptill, were no pushovers, so Virat made a mark that mattered.

A pleasant 'surprise'

Vengsarkar was so impressed with Virat's batting skills that he believed that the time had come for him to represent India and show his calibre at the highest level. Later, Virat acknowledged Vengsarkar's role in his growth and in persuading him to open the innings during the Emerging Players' tournament. Before this, Virat was mostly batting down the order and scoring in single digits. In the first match against South Africa, he scored just 2 and in the second match against Australian he made 1 run. That was why he was not given a chance in the third match.

With a century as an opener, Virat's confidence shot up to the next level. He finished the series with a half-century against a South African side, which was fortified with the fiery bowling pair of Lonwabo Tsotsobe and Wayne Parnell. In this tournament, Virat made a total of 204 runs with an average of 51 and was the second highest run-getter for his team, after Shikhar Dhawan. With this kind of run gathering, it was very difficult for the selectors to ignore Virat for the next series.

Just after this tournament, the selection committee, led by Vengsarkar, met to pick the Test and ODI squads for the Sri Lanka tour in August 2008. India was to play five ODIs against the home team Sri Lanka in the Idea Cup. Vengsarkar suggested Virat's name, and Virat finally got his debut opportunity in the national squad.

Today, the two star players picked by Vengsarkar, Virat and Dhoni, may be great teammates, but the scenario was not the same in 2008. When Virat's name came up for selection in the Idea Cup, the then Indian skipper Dhoni resisted it. So did the team coach Gary Kirsten. They wanted to keep the existing team going, as they had not seen Virat play. It is believed that the team management's first choice was S. Badrinath, who had a great domestic season that year, but the Colonel stood his ground and the other selectors also backed him.

Virat boarded the flight to Sri Lanka. Before the Sri Lankan tour, he had played only eight List A matches, and his selection was labelled a 'surprise call-up'.

The bilateral series of three Tests and five ODIs was played between hosts Sri Lanka and India. The Test matches started in the last week of July and the ODIs, for which Virat was selected, began on 18 August (one of the 18s said to be connected to his jersey number, though Virat has said that it was the number given to him when he played in the ICC U-19 World Cup in 2008 and he continued playing with the same number).

Interestingly, because Sachin Tendulkar pulled out of the ODIs because of an injury, Badrinath too made his debut in the same ODI series. However, he played only six more ODIs and a couple of Tests after that.

Meanwhile, Vengsarkar had handed Virat his first seat on the national team, the dream of every Indian cricketer, and Virat was all set to make the most of this opportunity.

⭐ Virat is the first ever batsman to score double hundreds in four consecutive Test series. He achieved the feat against West Indies, England, New Zealand and Bangladesh.

6

The boy who debuted at Dambulla

The date 18 August 2008 holds a special place in the history of Indian cricket. Looking back, this number eighteen only added to the stories around Virat's jersey number, which is also eighteen.

The teenager joined the playing XI as an opener who would temporarily replace one of the feared pair – Sachin Tendulkar or Virender Sehwag. Sachin had suffered an injury during the third Test of the Sri Lanka series (played before the one-dayers) and so had Sehwag during the practice session on the eve of the first ODI. 'Captain Cool' M.S. Dhoni lost two of his best batsmen in one go, and that too before the first match of the ODI series. He had to find a solid opening combination quickly. Despite having more experience than Virat, Badrinath had not batted at the top of the order. Dhoni decided to play Virat in the first match, based on his success as an opener in the recent Emerging Players tournament.

Virat had not even taken part in the warm-up match before the ODI series, and there he was in one of the toughest positions in the order, trying to fit into the glorious and giant mantle of Sachin or Sehwag. It was enough to rattle any veteran, let alone a teenager.

And so it came to pass that a passionate and still-chubby batsman, who had led India to the U-19 World Cup victory only a few months before his launch on the international platform, walked into the grounds of Dambulla. As he began the game with Gautam Gambhir at the other end, young Virat looked out of sorts and visibly nervous. It was his first match, and as a middle-order batsman he was not used to facing new balls. Often the ball moved faster than he expected, and he ended up missing many balls.

Virat faced the first ball of his national team career from the all-time Sri Lankan great Chaminda Vaas. The outstanding left arm bowler – who still holds the record for the best bowling figures in ODI history – tested the teenager with his stock ball, the one that angled across the right-hander and then straightened, usually foxing him. Virat defended, with his bat close to the front pad. In the third ball of the seventh over, Virat leaned forward and flicked Vaas into square leg for a four. And that first four in his international career seemed to boost his confidence.

In the next over, Virat faced Nuwan Kulasekara, another dangerous swing bowler. He pitched the ball on a good length just outside the off stump. Virat was unsure whether to go forward or back, and was struck outside the line of off stump by a ball and given an lbw.

So Virat's much anticipated debut match came to an abrupt end. He had stayed on the crease for 33 minutes, faced 22 balls and scored a paltry 12 runs. Finally, India was all out for just 146. Sri Lanka won the match by 8 wickets.

Virat stuck around for the rest of the series as a makeshift opener. He batted better in the second game at the same venue two days later, scoring 37 runs. In his fourth match, he scored his first ODI half-century, a score of 54 runs. India won that match by 3 wickets, eventually winning the series 3–2. It was India's first ODI series win against Sri Lanka on their home ground. In this series, Virat scored a total of 159 runs with an average of 31.8.

Cricketer Harbhajan Singh, who also played in that series, recalls Virat's debut. 'I remember when Virat came to Sri Lanka,' he says, 'none of the stalwart players was able to read Ajantha Mendis's bowling well. But Virat was keen to get into the middle and prove a point to him.'

His scorecard was increasing only gradually, but Virat was already scoring on full-on aggression. A member of the team's support staff is reported to have commented,

'*Jumma jumma do* match *khela heh, lekin* attitude *aur* arrogance *to dekho* (He has played just about two matches but look at his attitude and arrogance)!'

Virat was like that; still is. His attitude makes him what he is. As his former teammate Nehra says, 'He always tries to motivate himself through his aggression.' Nehra also feels that Virat's aggression is a secondary concern as long as he scores runs and does not violate the ICC Code of Conduct.

Attitude can, of course, be a player's unique strength. Former Indian U-19 team coach believes that the best thing about him is that he *hates* getting out. 'He always loved to stay on the wicket,' Rajput says. 'He was very, very serious about his game. Whenever he got out, we saw him coming back to the dressing room and throwing his bat and gloves down in frustration.'

'Dear Virat Kohli, Can you please stop making batting look so easy, it's embarrassing for most other batters in the world. Thanks.'

AARON FINCH,
Australian international
cricketer in a tweet

In the grip of uncertainty

Getting out was not the only reality that was going to bite young Virat on this rocky path. The two openers, Sachin and Sehwag, recovered and came back, and Virat was dropped from the national squad after the Idea Cup.

His next opportunity came during the home ODI series against England in November 2008. But as Sachin and Sehwag were back, there was no slot for him to play and he had to sit it out on the bench. However, the good thing was that he got a BCCI Grade D contract at the end of 2008, ensuring him a reasonably good regular sum a year.

When a player plays domestic cricket, he or she is paid per match and the amount is not a lot either. Once selected to represent the country, the player gets a yearly contract with a payment package, irrespective of whether one plays a series or gets dropped. After his father's death in 2006, his Rs 15-lakh contract was a breather, and it possibly helped him concentrate further on his cricket.

Virat was not a regular member of the Indian team, but he continued to excel on the domestic front. That's why he got selected again for the four-nation Emerging Players tournament in July–August 2009 in Australia.

He opened the innings for India and emerged as the highest scorer for the team in the tournament, with 398 runs from seven matches, at an average of 66.32. In the Indian final against South Africa, Virat scored his second century of the tournament and helped India win the match by 17 runs and lift the trophy.

In the following press conference, chief selector and cricketing legend Krishnamachari Srikkanth acknowledged that Virat was outstanding and that the shots he had played spoke volumes about his ability. Virat too marked this tournament as the turning point in his career.

His confidence was high, he was mentally stronger, he was focused, and he had learnt to bat in pressure conditions. With his two centuries and two fifties in the tournament, Virat ensured that he remained fresh in the selectors' minds.

They had no reason not to give Virat another go. He was selected for the Compaq Cup, a triangular series featuring New Zealand and hosts Sri Lanka in September 2009. Virat was returning to the squad after a gap of nearly twelve months.

Each team was to play two ODI matches and the best two teams would face off in the final. Initially, Virat was not selected for the tournament. But Sehwag's absence due to a shoulder injury and Gambhir's groin injury left India with a headache and two empty slots.

Virat didn't play the first two matches as Dinesh Karthik was used as a replacement opener. Karthik failed with the bat and, in the finals, the team decided to give Virat a chance. The pressure was on Dhoni to use him as an opener, but the Indian skipper was aware that Virat was not a regular opener, so he had him bat in the middle order. As Sachin played a magnificent innings of 138 runs to help India win the trophy, Virat only got to face two balls and scored as many runs.

A golden chance

It looked like Virat was becoming somewhat of a substitute batsman, replacing injured players. His next assignment was the ICC Champions Trophy in South Africa, where once again he came in to replace quick-fire all-rounder Yuvraj Singh, who had broken a finger during fielding practice. As they say, sometimes life gives you a second chance, but it's what you do with it that counts.

Virat had yet another opportunity to show his mettle – that too in a prestigious ICC event – and he grabbed it with both hands!

As it turned out, he failed in India's first match against arch-rivals Pakistan, scoring only 16 runs. But in the second match against West Indies, he notched up an under-pressure, classy, unbeaten 79 runs at the Centurion grounds in Gauteng, which won him his very first Man of the Match award. The twenty-one-year-old had started repaying the faith placed in him.

After that, Virat's runs began to flow both at the domestic level and in international matches. He made his first ODI century against Sri Lanka in December 2009 in Kolkata, which was the first of his many brilliant knocks in run chases. Virat was beginning to believe that he belonged in the Indian team.

He followed the Kolkata performance up with brilliant scores of 91 and 71 in the tri-series ODI tournament in Dhaka, involving Sri Lanka and Bangladesh. Virat, the now flamboyant right-hander, displaying a very solid temperament, scored his second hundred and his first one against Bangladesh. Not only was he declared the most consistent contributor in that tournament, but the fact that he got 102 runs off 95 balls helped him bag his career's second Man of the Match award.

It was clear that Virat had cemented a permanent place in the Indian team. It wasn't long before he started hitting the headlines, too, and producing staggering numbers in all formats of the game. He began to set a golden standard in consistency, both at home and away matches. Indian cricket had acquired an indispensable player who was rising in stature with every game.

Virat's hunger for runs has only grown over the years, says Harbhajan Singh. 'There was never any lack of talent in him,' says Singh, 'but he showed that one can achieve anything through hard work.' Interestingly, there were five other players – Manoj Tiwary, Yusuf Pathan, Manpreet Gony, Pragyan Ojha, and S. Badrinath – who made their ODI debuts in the same year as Virat, but it was Virat who went on to blaze the most dazzling trail.

In 2017, nine years after making his ODI debut, Virat was back in Dambulla as Team India's captain and superstar. The BCCI tweeted a photo of Virat sitting on the same chair he had once sat in as a debutant years ago, but this time he had both his hands up in victory signs. And why not?

Virat reached 25 Test hundreds in 127 innings, second only to legendary Australian cricketer Sir Don Bradman, who completed the feat in 68 innings.

Virat scored 102 against the West Indies in the Tri-Series in 2013 and was chosen Man of the Match for his match-winning innings

7

The boy who eyed the World Cup

Breaking into the Indian national cricket team is a tough job indeed, but maintaining that place is even more difficult. Virat soon realized this as his initial years in the squad were turning out to be a mixed bag. He also had no fixed position in the batting order. Whether he was batting at number three or down the order at number seven depended on the match situation and what the team needed. This made the task of cementing a place in the Indian team even more challenging for him.

Meanwhile, the World Cup was calling.

The ICC World Cup is a floodlit opportunity for a cricketing nation to announce its supremacy once in four years. The year 2011 was big for Indian cricket as the ICC World Cup was scheduled to be held on the Indian subcontinent, with co-hosts Sri Lanka and Bangladesh.

Along with a billion plus cricket fans in the home crowd, the Indian team was eagerly wishing to lift the trophy.

India's first and only win in the ODI World Cup had been in 1983 when the legendary 'Kapil's Devils' became champions in England. Ever since, the greats of Indian cricket, like Sachin Tendulkar, Rahul Dravid, Sourav Ganguly, Mohammad Azharuddin, Anil Kumble, and V.V.S. Laxman, had not had another opportunity to hold the coveted trophy. In the 2007 World Cup held in the Caribbean, India had been rudely knocked out of the tournament in the first round itself. So they were expected to make amends in 2011. The Indian team had won many tough series and trophies after that, but this one, the most hallowed, the most beloved, was missing from the cabinet.

Against this emotionally charged backdrop, only the very best could aspire to find a well-earned place in the Indian team for the World Cup.

Finding no. 4

The Indian lineup was as impressive as ever. With the likes of Sachin Tendulkar and Virender Sehwag opening the innings, followed ably by Gautam Gambhir, Suresh

Raina, Yuvraj Singh, and M.S. Dhoni – the batting side was full of explosive firepower. However, there was one slot in the batting line-up – the crucial number four position – that was not written in stone yet.

Initially, Dhoni was not very confident about selecting Virat for that slot. He had another player in mind and, once again, it was S. Badrinath. But Virat had consistently been staking his claim for the position with a string of important, in-your-face knocks.

Growing up, Virat had idolized Sachin Tendulkar as a batsman. He had often dreamed of playing alongside legends like Sachin and Sehwag, while wearing the Indian jersey. In 2009, Virat got a wonderful chance to prove himself in front of his heroes.

The stage could not have been better set than at Kolkata's historic Eden Gardens. India was playing Sri Lanka and the visitors, batting first, put up an imposing 315 runs on the board. However, India unfortunately lost openers Sehwag and Tendulkar cheaply when the score was only 22 runs. It was left to Gautam Gambhir to play a leading knock, but even he needed some support at the other end. Coming in at number four, Virat proved to be the perfect foil for Gambhir. The two put up a stand of 224 runs for the third wicket, with both hitting centuries. Virat jumped in the air with joy and raised his bat as he completed his first ODI century.

Those applauding his knock in the dressing room included Indian seamer Ashish Nehra. 'After we lost those two big wickets, the atmosphere in the dressing room was quite sombre because we were chasing an intimidating total,' he recalls. 'We all well knew Gautam's calibre, but was this young boy up to the mark? Well, Virat soon proved that he belonged there, at the number four position.'

Virat hit his second ODI ton in Bangladesh next year. Chasing 248 to win against the hosts, he proved to be the fulcrum of Indian batting as he ensured that the team sailed through, riding on his solid knock of 102 not out.

However, Virat's first two ODI centuries, crucial as they had been, were against relatively weaker sides – Sri Lanka and Bangladesh. He still had a lot to prove. But could he?

Chasing targets

After that knock in Bangladesh, Virat dwindled into a mixed phase as he hit a few 50s but also got out with a meagre run collection on as many occasions. Following his 102 against Bangladesh, he was out for a mere 2 runs against Sri Lanka in the very next match. He scored two 50s in Zimbabwe in May 2010, but there were also scores of 0 and 18 in the same series.

Virat's big moment to prove himself beyond the shadow of doubt came in Sri Lanka in 2010.

As luck would have it, in the seven innings that he played in the Asia Cup, with India, Pakistan, Sri Lanka, and Bangladesh competing, and in the Triangular Series in Sri Lanka, with India, New Zealand and Sri Lanka playing, Virat could only score a total of around 100 runs (67 in the Asia Cup and 37 in the Triangular series). Pressure was building up on him to perform consistently and effectively. So, when Australia arrived in India in the winter of 2010 to play three ODIs and two Test matches, it was seen as the first big-time test for Virat's batsmanship – one that would cement his place in the Indian side.

The first ODI in Kochi was washed out, and the teams travelled to Visakhapatnam for the second ODI at the Dr Y.S. Rajasekhara Reddy ACA–VDCA Cricket Stadium. In this match, Australia put up a daunting 292 runs on a track that suited the batsmen and slower bowlers. Chasing that mammoth score to win, Virat, playing at number three, was on the crease in the first over itself as opener Shikhar Dhawan fell for a nought.

Virat was under pressure to score. He hadn't been able to push the ball through the gaps in recent outings, and this was an innings that was under the microscopic observation of chief selector Krishnamachari Srikkanth.

This time round, Virat stitched an important 137-run partnership with Yuvraj Singh for the third wicket and steadied the Indian ship. Virat and Raina then added another 84 runs before Virat was snared by James Hopes off a ball by John Hastings. By then, Virat had scored 118 runs in 121 balls, laced with 11 fours and a six. His effort won the match for India, and for him, an important Man of the Match award.

Virat said in a press conference after the match, 'I had not scored in the last six to seven matches. I was under pressure. I was not hitting in the gaps. It was very satisfying, and it gives you a lot of confidence when you score chasing under pressure. I will not say my place is cemented. I have to keep performing well in few more chases.'[8]

> 'Virat is the best shorter version batsman that I have ever seen. He's been an absolute genius.'
>
> **KUMAR SANGAKKARA, former cricketer and captain of the Sri Lankan national team**

This was a landmark match for Virat. Not only did he defeat all the demons in his own mind, but he also looked set on a mission of winning matches for the country while chasing. If one examines his success rate, all his three ODI tons had come while chasing.

Virat went on to say, 'You try to learn from the mistakes. You tend to fail sometimes. This is part and parcel of the game. You do the basics right and train hard; it pays back.'⁹

It certainly did for a much-relieved Srikkanth. After the match, he said that the win was important for India as it had involved chasing down a record total against a world number one side. Without naming Virat, he said that the successful chase underlined India's bench strength going into the World Cup.

Virat's fate was still a puzzle as far as the World Cup was concerned. However, his confidence was soaring, and his form had returned. He struck yet another ton in the very next match against New Zealand in Guwahati. Here, too, his gritty nature and his gumption for a fight were on full display.

Guwahati usually has a relatively earlier morning start and that helps the seamers initially. The Kiwis were swinging left and right, and Virat had to put his head down and build his innings. His other teammates – Gambhir, Murali Vijay and Yuvraj – produced flashier, stroke-filled innings, while Virat looked for ones and twos, and the occasional boundaries. Still, Virat's score was not slow as he ran really hard between the wickets and played intelligent cricket. When his century was completed, the celebration was not as passionate and full of fury as earlier; rather, it showed an assured Virat who seemed to be aware of his place in the Indian side. In the next two matches against the Kiwis, Virat scored two 50s to add to his growing stature in the Indian team.

In 2010, Virat finished with 995 runs in twenty-five matches. He stood just behind Hashim Amla of South Africa who hit 1,058 runs that year and was the leading run scorer in ODIs in the world. It looked like Virat had arrived on the international scene. But had he come to stay and shine in the World Cup?

Virat broke the world record for playing the most innings before recording a duck in T20 internationals. He recorded his maiden T20I duck after 47 innings, playing in his 52nd T20I match.

8

The boy who earned his place in the World Cup

Virat had found his feet and proved himself with two big knocks in 2010, but there was still a fair bit of scrambling left to solve the jigsaw puzzle of the playing XI in the 2011 World Cup. When the fifteen-men squad for the World Cup was announced, Virat was in it.

Harbhajan Singh, an important member of the Indian side then, was closely watching Virat's progress. 'I would not give the captain credit for Virat's selection,' he says. 'In fact, Virat selected himself for the World Cup with his performance. He did so well from 2009 to 2011 that skipper Dhoni *had* to find a place for him in the side.'

Being part of the World Cup at such an early age – Virat was only twenty-two then – was no mean achievement. 'Playing in the World Cup is a big moment for anyone who wants to play for the country,' adds Harbhajan

Singh. 'He was a young kid with minimal experience and was playing with the greats like Sachin, Sehwag, Dhoni and Yuvraj at their best. Being a part of this team and playing with such legends must have been a big thing for Virat.'

Virat was part of the team, but he still needed to ensure his place and batting position in the playing XI. He had scored most of his big knocks coming in at number three, but that place was not to be his. India was looking to open with Sachin Tendulkar and Virender Sehwag, with Gautam Gambhir dropping to number three. Along with Suresh Raina and Yuvraj Singh, Virat could stake a claim for the number four position. And in skipper Dhoni's mind, this contest for the number four position was a 'slot-war' and the player best suited would win.

In the year preceding the World Cup, Yuvraj Singh was not playing in every match due to health issues. The competition for the number four position was between Virat and Suresh Raina. The left-handed Raina was a close associate of M.S. Dhoni in many run chases for the Indian team as well as for Chennai Super Kings, the IPL team they both represented.

However, Virat had made sure that he could not be ignored. As if to prove his point, in a practice game in Chennai against New Zealand before the World Cup, Virat hit a strong 59 runs.

Dhoni was slowly realizing that Virat was suited to fill the number four position because he could build a long innings; Raina could come in later and do the job of a finisher. After India beat New Zealand in that warm-up game, Dhoni said to the press, 'It is the number four slot where Kohli needs to bat, with Gautam Gambhir at number three. To perform to his potential, Virat needs to bat up the order... Raina can score batting down the order as well and he has done very well batting at number five and six. So it will be a slot war more than for a place in the playing XI.'[10]

In this match, Virat had hit another 50 and now Dhoni was certain that he held an edge over Raina. South African great Gary Kirsten was the Indian team's coach during the 2011 World Cup. He later said that with the kind of form and attitude Virat brought to the side, picking him was an easy decision. In 2008, Kirsten said to the press, 'Any guy with half a cricket eye would have known that he was going to

'I think Virat has a GPS fitted in his mind. He can pick the gaps so easily.'

HARSHA BHOGLE,
Indian cricket
commentator and
journalist

be a great player. His hunger for runs, his ball-striking ability…. He hit the ball to all parts of the ground, got natural power and then the determination to go with it. He had the hunger to be great.'[11]

Ashish Nehra, senior strike bowler with the World Cup team, was also certain that Virat was cut out for the big league: 'The team was filled with titans like Sachin, Sehwag, Gambhir and Yuvraj, but Kohli still made a place for himself. I knew him from the Delhi Ranji side days, so we gelled nicely, and we would have light, funny conversations.'

The World Cup begins

India's first match in the 2011 World Cup was against Bangladesh in Dhaka. There was some history to this contest.

Much has been written about India–Pakistan rivalry in cricket and we all know how intense and heated it can get. However, not many would have experienced the kind of frenzy Bangladesh fans generate when their team is playing against India, and especially when India loses.

One example is from Dhaka in 2004 during M.S. Dhoni's debut series. India were beaten by Bangladesh in the second match, giving the hosts their first-ever win over India. Commentator Ravi Shastri described the 'war dance' as the jubilant Bangladeshi players celebrated their victory after the last Indian wicket fell. Outside the ground, it was quite a scene too. The streets surrounding the Bangabandhu National Stadium in Dhaka were filled with lakhs of people – all circling the stadium and passionately chanting 'Bangladesh, Bangladesh'. It was as if the entire city had erupted in that moment.

The second big win for Bangladesh came in the 2007 World Cup in the West Indies. The Indian team was unceremoniously knocked out in the first round. The architects of this loss were none other than Bangladesh. Indian fans were confident that their team would easily win the game, but instead India lost to Bangladesh by 5 wickets. There were only four or five journalists from Bangladesh in the press box, but the kind of noise they made was unbelievable. With every run taken by the Bangladesh team, their fervour reached a higher level. By the time Bangladesh won, a few of the journalists were jumping on their desks in celebration. And why not? This was a big victory for Bangladesh because they had knocked out a tournament favourite in the very first round.

So, when the two teams squared off in 2011, Indian fans and cricketers had disappointing memories feeding their passion.

India batted first and put up a mammoth 370 on the board. The irrepressible Virender Sehwag hit 175 runs off 140 balls. Virat, batting at number four, added a double-century partnership with Sehwag. In the course of this, Virat scored an unbeaten dream century in his debut at the World Cup.

Bangladesh fell short by 87 runs as India made a winning start to the campaign. After the match, skipper Dhoni singled out Sehwag and Virat for their efforts in ensuring India's victory. Dhoni emphasized that this was a display of responsible batting as India first put up a good opening partnership and then built on it to mount an attack in the end overs.

In the second match against England, Yuvraj Singh returned to the side and batted at number four. Virat was dropped to the seventh spot, possibly because the team needed a quick run collection by the likes of Yusuf Pathan and Yuvraj Singh. As a result, Virat could not get in much batting. This was again a high-scoring, high-tension match that ended in a tie – both India and England scored 338 runs!

It's India's Cup

In the next match, against Ireland, Virat – once again occupying the number four slot – scored a useful 34. It was evident that Dhoni was trying to accommodate both Yuvraj and Virat in the side and give them enough batting overs. In the last group match, India faced the West Indies and Virat played at number three while Yuvraj came in at number four. The two put up a partnership of 120 runs as Virat compiled an important 50 and Yuvraj went on to register a match-winning century.

In the next contest, Virat got a start against Australia in the quarter-final but was out cheaply against Pakistan in the semi-final. However, India won both the matches due to a strong display by Yuvraj, Sachin, Gambhir, and Dhoni.

The grand tale of the 2011 World Cup win is often told and repeated untiringly. In the final, India defeated Sri Lanka by 6 wickets, to lift the World Cup for the second time. Everyone remembers the 'helicopter shot' by Dhoni that fetched the final winning runs for India. But Virat too had an important role to play in that match, after India had lost early wickets.

'In that innings, Viru [Sehwag] and Sachin were out early,' recalls Harbhajan Singh. 'Gautam was playing well and Virat, the newcomer, joined him in the middle. With so much pressure on him, the way Virat handled it was very crucial. His 85-run partnership with Gautam showed the great fighting character of this youngster. Dilshan [Tillakaratne] took a brilliant catch, otherwise it could well have been another hundred for Virat.'

India lifted the trophy at the Wankhede Stadium in Mumbai and Virat carried Sachin Tendulkar on his shoulders, all to a standing ovation. Virat dedicated the win to his childhood idol Sachin, saying, 'He carried the burden of the nation for twenty-one years, so it is time we carried him on our shoulders.'

It was Sachin Tendulkar's last World Cup, and Virat Kohli's first.

Becoming a world champion at twenty-two is no small triumph. But what does one do after that? Rest on one's laurels or aspire for more? Virat chose the second route and decided that from then on, he only wanted to be the best in the world.

In an interview a few years later, Virat spoke on *Sportskeeda* about what he learned from the World Cup: 'I gained a lot of confidence from that World Cup. In my very first World Cup, I was part of the triumphant squad.... It gave me confidence from the fact that we had achieved something special…. I couldn't really connect to the kind of emotion that all the other senior players had because they hadn't won it for so long. To see all that emotion come out…I really understood the importance of a cricket World Cup.'[12]

Now he wanted to conquer every challenge that came his way. Remembering that day, Virat told BCCI. TV in 2015: 'From that day on, maybe even before that, I always wanted to be the best player in the world. I wanted to be among the best players that people would speak about. I always wanted to be a player that will be known even when I finished my career as a cricketer. I never wanted to be on the sidelines or be one of the players in the side.'[13]

It is said that 'the bigger the challenge, the better the opportunity for growth'. Virat matched this truism perfectly, size for size, as he moved ahead rapidly in the legions of world cricket.

Virat has the most number of 50+ scores in T20 internationals. He has gone past the 50-run mark on 20 occasions, a record shared only by Rohit Sharma.

9

The boy who was
hungry for challenges

No cricket ground in the world had as fast or bouncy a pitch then – a graveyard for batsmen – as the Western Australian Cricket Association (WACA) Ground in Perth, Australia. Cricket happens too soon and too quickly on this pitch. Manic fans scream in the sun-sizzled stands, baying for blood, chanting the names of aggressive bowlers bowling a toe-crushing yorker or a sharp bouncer aimed at the heads of unsuspecting batsmen. The best cricketers have been challenged here. India too has had a poor record on this ground, having lost 75 per cent of the Test matches they have played here.

There have been memorable knocks, though. Mohinder Amarnath's immortal 100 and 90 in 1978, Sunil Gavaskar's century also in the same year, and Rahul Dravid and V.V.S. Laxman's match-winning 50s in 2008. But none were as emphatic as the 114 made by eighteen-year-old Sachin Tendulkar in 1992. Sachin took the likes of Craig McDermott and Mike Whitney to all corners of the park in an innings laced with 16 boundaries. Australian spearhead Craig McDermott said after the match: 'This bloke could do so much at eighteen, I wonder what he will do when he turns twenty-five.' We all know what Sachin did later. McDermott's prophecy was not unfounded because if a batsman could score at WACA, he could do that anywhere in the world.

So, when Virat arrived in Perth for the third Test match of the 2012 series, he was well aware of the importance of the setting.

Sachin Tendulkar also came to bat in this series at WACA. It was amusing to note that three of the four pacers who bowled to Sachin twenty years ago were still present in the stadium that day but in different roles! Paul Reiffel, who debuted in the 1992 series, was one of the umpires in the game while Craig McDermott was Australia's bowling coach. Merv Hughes, a fearsome bowler in his time, whose trademark handlebar moustache was supposedly insured for $370,000 in his heydays as a member of the Australian national team, was working as a tour guide with a famous Australian sports tour company. And Mike Whitney had become a TV presenter hosting popular shows and also had a side gig as a tambourine player in his own band. While the bowlers had all retired from cricket, Sachin was still strolling out to bat to a standing ovation.

Virat could not miss the respect and awe that Sachin still evoked. He knew it was crucial to score big runs Down Under to earn the respect of bowlers worldwide.

However, it wasn't the best time for the famed Indian batting line-up. Sachin Tendulkar, Rahul Dravid, V.V.S. Laxman, and Virender Sehwag were easily tamed by Australian bowlers. India had lost the first two Test matches when they arrived in Perth, and the Indians were bundled out for 161 in the first innings. Virat was, in fact, the top scorer with his 44 off 81 balls. Australia managed a 200-plus lead and the Indian team was once again under duress on this fast wicket. The story was no different in the second innings, but for Virat, who scored 75 and was once again the highest run-getter for India.

This came as no surprise to the likes of Harbhajan Singh and coach Rajkumar Sharma. Harbhajan says, 'Virat would become an even more dangerous player on wickets that were difficult to bat on.' Coach Sharma always underlined Virat's appetite for challenges, and this was evident in Perth once again.

Virat followed up these two significant knocks in Perth with a century – 116 runs – in Adelaide in the next Test match. This was the only century scored by an Indian batsman in the series. The Indian media cheered their new hero, while the Australian press acknowledged the passing on of the batting baton. It seemed clear that the fort would no longer be held by the likes of Tendulkar or Dravid but by a certain Virat Kohli.

This was the last Test match for Rahul Dravid, one of the world's greatest cricketers, as he announced his retirement. Virat was the highest run-scorer for India in Perth, with a total of 300 runs in the Test series, ahead of Sachin Tendulkar's series total of 287.

Virat's score of 116 in Adelaide was his first Test century, and it was in his eighth Test match. By this time, Virat was already an established ODI player with 75 matches, 8 centuries and a World Cup to boast. But 'real' cricket was still Test cricket. It was this format of five gruelling days that

measured a player's skills and mental strength. In the last two matches of the series, Virat had scored well and appeared to be the most comfortable batsman in the Indian line-up. From now on, it was Virat who would be India's bastion of

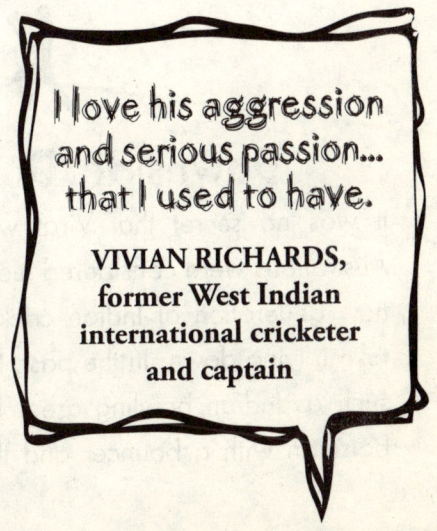

I love his aggression and serious passion... that I used to have.

VIVIAN RICHARDS,
former West Indian
international cricketer
and captain

hope and victory. At the time, Australian channel ABC News wrote that Virat Kohli was the only bright spot in the Indian side that lost 4–0 to the hosts.[14]

Another innings that became the talking point of the series came in the Tri-nation one-day trophy, played after the Tests in Australia. In a game against Sri Lanka, India were 86 for 2 wickets, chasing 321 runs for victory. Virat came to the crease and scored a whirlwind 133 in just 86 balls to help India win the match with 13 overs remaining. Australian cricketer Dean Jones described this innings as 'one of the greatest ODI knocks of all time'.[15]

However, while Virat left a strong impression on the Australian bowlers and the cricket fans with his batting, he was also criticized by opponents and fans for his behaviour on the field.

Downside, Down Under

It was no secret that Virat was far from meek. The Australians were considered masters of sledging, but the new generation of Indian cricketers were not going to take it lying down. In the past, there had been instances such as Indian bowling great Javagal Srinath hitting a batsman with a bouncer and then approaching him in a gentlemanly fashion to enquire if he was fine, only to be sent back with the choicest of remarks. But, if sledged by opponents, Virat returned fire right back. During the series, the Australian media wrote that Virat's behaviour was boorish, while the Indian team and Virat thought that they were only giving back as good as they got.

However, there was one incident that crossed the line, and Virat too admitted his mistake later. During the second Test match of the series in Sydney, the Australians were piling up runs and Virat was fielding near the boundary. He was booed by the crowd, which shouted out nasty remarks about him and his family. Virat did the unbelievable – he made a rude gesture to the crowd.

This regrettable picture was splashed on the front page of newspapers the next morning. Match referee Ranjan Madugalle from Sri Lanka had missed the incident and saw it in the papers. This was a serious matter and could have attracted a heavy penalty and maybe even a ban for a few matches. He called in Virat, who immediately apologized. He was fined 50 per cent of his match fee and many felt that he was lucky to get away lightly.

Australian batsman and former captain Michael Clarke remembers the incident too, but to him it was a reflection of the changing attitude of the Indian cricket team that refused to be kept down. 'Virat was full of confidence and energy,' says Clarke. 'His passion for representing

India was something that always stood out. He would have done things in his young days that he won't today. But he wanted to send a message to the opponents and the crowd that they should treat the Indian team with respect, and they cannot walk over them.'

Out of Line

Team India captain Virat Kohli has had his share of controversies besides the hand-gesture one at the Sydney Cricket Ground in Australia. In 2015, he breached the BCCI's code of conduct by inviting his girlfriend Anushka Sharma to the pavilion during a washed–out game and was handed a warning by the board. In the same year, he lashed out at a journalist for writing an article on him and Anushka (later, he found out that he had targeted the wrong person and apologized). His altercation with Gautam Gambhir during the IPL in 2013 in the middle of a match between Royal Challengers Bangalore and Kolkata Knight Riders (KKR) needed the intervention of the players and the umpires, and his rift with the then India cricket coach Anil Kumble, which ended in the latter's resignation in June 2017, earned him criticism. In November

2018, Virat landed in another controversy for asking a cricket fan to 'leave India' because he had said that he liked Australian and English batsmen over Indians.

Clarke adds, 'Sourav Ganguly set the tone for the Indian cricket team that nobody could treat them with disrespect or walk over them. Virat has taken it to the next level. The confidence he reflects has rubbed off onto the younger players, too, and today the Indian team is very different.'

Virat also had another person drilling sense into him – Coach Sharma recalls regularly talking to Virat while he was on this Australia tour, about his batting and other issues. Sharma was a person Virat never wanted to disappoint. Virat later admitted that the incident was something he would like to put behind him.

With runs ticking away on his personal scoreboard, Virat was consistently crossing milestones, But as the game's most common saying goes: 'Cricket by chance'. Virat was poised to speed up to the next level. Would he?

Virat is the only player in international cricket to average over 50 in all three formats – in Tests, ODIs and T20 internationals.

10

The boy who became captain and number one batsman

Virat was fast becoming the go-to man in one-day cricket for India, the player the team captain looked up to when tackling tough match situations. Even in Test cricket, in the Australian series, Virat demonstrated that he was ready to take his batting centre stage. He was the highest ODI scorer of the year in 2011 and won the prestigious ICC ODI Player of the Year award in 2012.

It was around 2011 and 2012 that Virat stepped up his fitness programme, taking it to the next level. Ashish Nehra, who played alongside Virat on the Delhi team and the Indian side, says, 'When he first came to the scene, he was a chubby-cheeked boy. He loved good food and tended to gain weight easily. But he started to work hard on his fitness. The amount of time he spent in the gym went up enormously.' Following the army adage – 'The more you sweat in peace, the less you bleed in war' – Virat worked out tirelessly to be physically and mentally alert all the time and to never let his intensity dip.

In 2012, Virat was made vice-captain of the Indian team for the Asia Cup. In cricket, a vice-captain is not much of a leadership role; it's mostly about filling in for the captain when he is not on the ground. However, the post signifies that the player is next in line for captaincy. The chairman of selectors, K. Srikkanth, said that the selectors saw strong leadership material in Virat and he was being groomed for the role.

Indeed, Virat had brought a fresh attitude to the team. West Indian legend and all-time great Vivian Richards too complimented Virat and perhaps paid him the highest honour by saying that Virat reminded him of himself. As part of Delhi Daredevils IPL team, Richards said in 2013 to PTI, 'I love watching Virat Kohli bat... I love his aggression, and serious passion that I used to have. He reminds me of myself... I love that as you can't teach these instinctive aspects.'[16]

Richards was not only impressed by Virat's batting but also by his attitude. He said, 'Just like me, he loves the ball to come to him. He wants to dive, stop the runs. He is a livewire unlike some fielders, who would just dig a hole and dive in it rather than dive to stop the ball.'[17]

Despite his next-level fitness regime and post of vice-captain, Virat had a mixed 2012 as he did not perform well in most of the matches against the visiting English side later that year. However, he came back with a sound 103 runs in the fourth Test match of the series.

In the one-dayers, however, Virat was unstoppable. He hit 183 against Pakistan in the Asia Cup and followed that up with two centuries against Sri Lanka. A tour of South Africa was coming up too. Historically, Indian teams and players that have excelled on foreign soils, especially in Australia, England, and South Africa, are considered truly successful. Virat showed his class in Australia and now it was his turn to prove the doubters wrong on the spongy, bouncy pitches of South Africa.

Rocking it in South Africa

Virat played his first Test match in South Africa in Johannesburg in December 2013. Batting at number four, he scored a wonderful 119 runs to help India put up a modest total of 280 runs in the first innings. In the second innings too Virat showed his batting prowess and missed another 100 by just 4 runs. These two knocks of 119 and 96 firmly established Virat as India's premier batsman even in Test cricket.

Batting in South Africa is not easy, especially for Indian batsmen who have grown up on slow and turning tracks. In South Africa, there is more bounce and sideways movement of the ball. Batsmen need to adjust their technique to counter hostile bowling on wickets supportive to the bowlers.

Virat had his plan ready. Over the years, he had built up a strong defence. Against the Proteas team, he evolved a slight adjustment of standing outside the crease. Staying strong on his desire to succeed, Virat managed to score big in South Africa. In fact, his century in Johannesburg was the first by any Indian at this venue in more than fifteen years, after Rahul Dravid in 1977!

Allan Donald, fearsome fast bowler of his time and bowling coach of South Africa, told PTI that Virat's disciplined innings reminded him of Sachin Tendulkar.[18]

Having conquered Australia and South Africa with his flawless batting, Virat now needed to succeed in England – a team against whom he had a poor record in Tests. The opportunity soon came when India toured England in the summer of 2014.

Unfortunately, it turned out to be a bleak series for India. Dhoni's men lost 3–1 to England despite leading

1–0 after two Tests. Virat had a forgettable series as a batsman. He scored at 13.40 in 10 innings and could not hit even a 50 once.

However, Test batting also depends on how well you are able to leave the deliveries outside the off stump. In this format, bowlers literally 'test' batsmen by bowling again and again outside the off stump with a strong slip cordon in place. (Slip fielders are placed behind the batsman on the offside of the field with the aim of catching an edged ball that is beyond the wicketkeeper's reach.) The idea is to tempt the batsman to play away-going deliveries and get caught out by the wicketkeeper or in the slips. Good Test batsmen are those who know when to leave deliveries outside the off stump and hence avoid the risk of getting out.

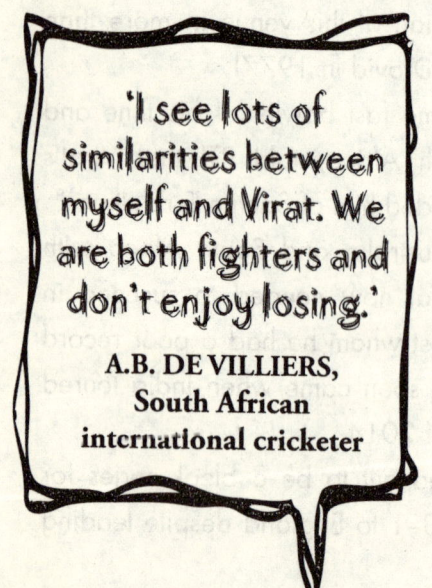

'I see lots of similarities between myself and Virat. We are both fighters and don't enjoy losing.'

A.B. DE VILLIERS,
South African
international cricketer

While Virat was able to play the deliveries from the middle of his bat, he was unsuccessful in leaving the ones he should have and was caught behind, chasing away-going deliveries. This was a major reason why he did not do very well in the England series.

Back in Oz

Despite a poor English summer, Virat was being counted among the top three batsmen in all forms of the game. After all, it was not in his nature to come second. An opportunity to surge ahead came in 2014 and 2015 when the Indian team toured Australia – where Virat had registered his first Test century two years ago in Perth.

Due to an injury, Dhoni was not playing in the first Test in Adelaide, and the captaincy fell on Virat's young – and ready – shoulders. The stand-in captain did an admirable job, scoring a century in the first innings. This was a ton he scored on debut as a captain, a proud record not held by many. But it soon became clear that Virat was not chasing personal records and the team's victory was his prime concern.

In the second innings, the Indian team had to score 364 runs on the last day to win. Usually, a 300-plus score on the last day of a Test match is not considered a feasible target to chase, but Virat took on the challenge and went after it.

When he came in to bat at number three, India's score was 57 for 2 wickets. There was a chance of India losing all the wickets and the match. It was not an easy decision to make, but Virat decided that his team would chase rather than play for a draw. He started to score quickly and found an able partner in Murali Vijay. The two added 185 runs in quick time and it seemed as though India might just win this improbable match. A large crowd of Indian fans was rooting for their team while an entire nation was glued to the TV, watching this fantastic display of cricket.

However, in an attempt to hasten the run rate, Vijay lost his wicket and that triggered a batting collapse. The Indian side was all out for 315. It was a huge disappointment because the Indian team was looking strong at 242 for the loss of 2 wickets before Vijay departed. Virat scored an epic 141 off 175 balls in this losing cause. India lost the match, but Virat won the hearts of the hard-to-please Australian fans and critics. After the match, Virat said that it was the best Test match he had ever played.

Virat's style of captaincy was also loud and clear. His aggressive leadership approach was all too clear as India looked to register wins abroad.

Dhoni returned for the next two matches as captain. Virat scored another century in Melbourne, the third Test match, with his personal best of 169 runs. He came in to bat again in the second innings with a fighting 50 to help India salvage a draw.

Immediately after the match, right in the middle of an important series, Dhoni announced his retirement from Test cricket. While he was planning ahead to focus on ODIs and T20s, he was also certain that India was in safe hands with Virat.

Virat underlined this with another century in the first innings of the last Test match. Having scored two tons in his debut Test, followed by this innings, Virat became the only batsman in the world to have scored three tons in his first three innings as a Test captain. He had made a total of 692 runs at an average of 87, with four centuries. No wonder he was named BCCI Player of the Year in 2015.

The series firmly decided the best Indian batsman in the world of cricket. And he answered to the name of Virat Kohli.

On 5 October 2018, Virat became the first cricket captain in the world to score 1000+ Test runs in three consecutive years.

11

The boy who chased 1 and 10,000

Firmly in control of the Indian Test side, one of the first objectives Virat wanted his team to achieve was winning overseas. The first stop was Sri Lanka. Four years had passed since India had won a Test series abroad (it was, in fact, during the India tour of Sri Lanka in 2015). It wasn't a great start to Virat's dream. Even though he scored a century in the first Test match, India lost the game and trailed 1–0 in the three-match series. However, a superb all-round performance by the team made India bounce back to claim the series 2–1, their first overseas win in four years!

Having tasted sweet victory, Virat's men demolished the visiting South African side 3–0 in the four-match series that followed. India was now the world's number two team in Test cricket, but Virat was eyeing the number one rank. Had he ever settled for anything but the best?

When India toured the West Indies in 2016, it was the first Test series for Virat in the Caribbean Islands. He celebrated his debut here with a superb 200 in Antigua. Strangely, this was Virat's first double hundred in a Test match; many thought it had come late for a batsman who had such a huge appetite for runs. Still, it was the first double ton by an Indian captain on foreign soil! India won the series comfortably at 2–0 (with two drawn matches) and this helped the Indian team reach the number one position in the ICC rankings for Test cricket.

Even though India was displaced by Pakistan briefly from the top position in August 2016, Virat and his men got it back as India whitewashed New Zealand 3–0 in a home series. Virat scored another double hundred in this series. And as if this was not enough, he scored double tons in the next two series against England and Bangladesh, becoming the first batsman to score double hundreds in four consecutive series. And whose record did he break? It was of the legendary Sir Donald Bradman and Rahul Dravid, both of whom had double hundreds in three consecutive series.

All through the noise of these personal records, Virat did not lose focus in making India an unbeatable team. The Indian side registered wins against Sri Lanka once again in December 2017 and Virat equalled Ricky Ponting's record of nine back-to-back Test series wins as captain. This was a great compliment for the team, led by Virat, as it matched the record set by a stupendous Australian team that had featured the likes of Ricky Ponting, Shane Warne, Glenn McGrath, Adam Gilchrist and Matthew Hayden. From the Sri Lankan series in 2015 to December 2017, India played thirty Test matches and won twenty-one, losing only two (the rest were draws).

The unmatchable one

The only blemish in Virat's captaincy career was not winning in England and Australia. Otherwise, during these years as captain, Virat established himself as the greatest contemporary batsman in all forms of the game and he also led India to become the number one team in Test cricket.

Meanwhile, Virat's own consistency at ODIs was becoming unmatchable and experts began to talk about him as one of the greatest one-day batsmen. They said that if Virat continued in the same vein, he could end up being the highest scorer in ODIs and be regarded as possibly the greatest ever in 50-over cricket.

In the 2015 ICC World Cup held in Australia and New Zealand, the Indian team was knocked out in the semi-final by the Australians. However, Virat shone as the highest scorer from the Indian side, scoring a smashing 100 in the opening match against Pakistan. Overall, 2015 was not the greatest year for Virat in ODIs as he averaged 37 – his lowest in the past seven years. But this was just an aberration because he scored 739 runs at an average of 92 in the following year.

In 2017, Virat was unstoppable. He scored a massive 1,460 runs at 76.84 runs per innings. If people thought that Virat had peaked, he surprised everyone with yet another stupendous year. In 2018, his best year so far, he scored more than 1,200 runs in ODIs, at an unbelievable average of 133.56. This kind of average is usually seen in a series or two, but maintaining the same rate for an

'On the field, he is aggressive, wears his heart on his sleeve, his body language can get out of control sometimes... I was the same.'

RICKY PONTING, former Australian cricketer and two-time World Cup winning captain

entire year catapulted Virat into a league of his own. He was scoring runs and breaking records in almost every innings, confidently nudging past greats like Brian Lara, Sanath Jayasuriya and Ricky Ponting.

One innings, in particular, made the cricket fraternity sit up and applaud Virat and acknowledge him as a master batsman. In October 2018, he crossed the 10,000-run mark in ODIs. He became the thirteenth batsman in the world to do so, but he was the *fastest* to get there. It took Virat only 205 innings to complete 10,000 runs; Sachin Tendulkar took 259 innings to achieve the same.

Virat was outstripping the competition and blazing a glorious trail. Australian all-rounder Glenn Maxwell paid a perfect tribute to Virat on the website Direct Hit: 'Name your format, name your conditions, and there's every chance Virat Kohli is the best batsman for the occasion… He's got an insatiable appetite for runs, for being the best at everything – the best fielder, the best fitness-wise, the best batter… He's got an incredible desire to just dominate.'[19]

And that's just what Virat was going to do in the Twenty20 format.

Among Indian skippers, Virat has won the most consecutive Test series as captain. Between 2015 and 2017, he led the Indian team to win nine consecutive series, equalling Australian Ricky Ponting's record for the same number of wins during 2005–08.

12

The boy who became a T20 and IPL superstar

Twenty20 cricket changed the dynamics of cricket. Coming decades after the first one-day match (in 1971), the Twenty20 (or T20) format was introduced by the England and Wales Cricket Board in 2003 for an inter-county tournament in England and Wales.

In a T20 game, the two teams play a single innings, each of a maximum of 20 overs. A game is usually completed in about three hours, with each innings being around 90 minutes long. There is a break of 10 minutes between the innings. This is a zippy, spectator- and viewer-friendly form of the game.

Now more than 80 leagues in this very popular format are being played all over the world. In the early years, India was not a big fan of this format as the BCCI thought that it would kill the 'purer' formats. But pressure from other countries and the ICC forced the Indian board to accept this format and they slowly started participating in T20 Internationals (T20Is).

To everyone's surprise India made global headlines when they won the inaugural edition of the World T20 in 2007 under the captainship of M.S. Dhoni. A year later, the T20 format grew a million-fold when the cash-rich IPL was launched with much fanfare by the BCCI. It was the perfect time for the Under-19 captain Virat to make an entry into the biggest cricket league of the world.

Virat's success in T20 too is the perfect example of talent and self-belief combined with hard work. With around 2,300 runs in T20Is and still going strong, he has a sizzling average of around more than 50. Today, he is also one of the costliest players in IPL. This short format has forced the batsmen to play all around the wicket as the number of balls is limited, and Virat remodelled himself for this game and found all the shots needed to succeed. His desire to perform and keep improving makes him one of the best batsmen in T20 cricket.

Tops in T20

Virat made his debut in the format in 2010 against Zimbabwe in Harare, but for the next two years he played only nine matches and did not perform very well in those early matches. In his tenth match, he scored his first half-century in T20. In his next match against New Zealand in Chennai, he scored 70 runs. Then he made another half-century against Afghanistan in the 2012 World T20 in Sri Lanka and got his first Man of the Match award in T20Is. After that, there was no looking back.

His commendable score of 78 not out in a crucial match against Pakistan won Virat another Man of the Match award. In that match, India had lost their first Super 8 encounter against Australia in the 2012 World T20 and they needed a win against Pakistan to stay alive in the tournament. Chasing a target of 129, India lost its top order too quickly. Virat scored a well-crafted 78 off just 61 balls and remained unbeaten to ensure India a place in the Super 8. It was one of his finest T20 innings, and one typically played under tremendous pressure.

Later, India crashed out of the World T20 championship in the Super 8 stage, but not before star batsman Virat had shown the world his class, especially when it came to the run chase during the tournament in Sri Lanka. Virat's innings against Pakistan made him a WhatsApp hero, with a popular joke going around: A Pakistan soldier tells his boss: '*Sahab, ab goli se nahi Kohli se dar lagta hai* (Boss, we don't fear the bullet now, but Kohli instead).'

Virat soon overtook New Zealand's cricketer Brendon McCullum to become the leading run scorer in chases in T20s. He also became the first Indian to complete 1,000 runs in T20Is. The Indian team played its first T20I match in 2005 and Virat made his debut in this format only in 2010, but he managed to reach the milestone before everyone else! He did it in only his twenty-seventh innings – five fewer than the previous record holders, England's Kevin Pietersen and Alex Hales, who reached it in their thirty-second innings.

In November 2018, Pakistan's Babar Azam broke Virat's record of the fastest 1,000 and reached the landmark in just 26 matches – one less than Virat. When compared to Virat, he surprised the media by saying his aim was to emulate Virat's performance in the cricketing arena. 'It's flattering to be compared to Kohli as he is very consistent, and his mindset is very good,' Azam said. '...he gives a 100-per cent every time he walks out to bat.... I am at the start of my career, so the aim is to be like him.'[20]

Virat was also the fastest to score 1,500 runs in T20I cricket.

> 'Virat is the best shorter version batsman that I have ever seen. He's been an absolute genius.'
>
> **KUMAR SANGAKKARA,**
> **former Sri Lankan**
> **cricketer and captain**

He added another feather in his cap after he became the fastest batsman to complete 2,000 runs in T20s because he took only 60 matches and 56 innings to enter the 2000 club. In comparison, his closest competition in the category, Brendon McCullum, took 71 matches and 66 innings.

Virat likes to keep pushing the boundaries. He is never content or complacent when it comes to hi game. He is in the all-time list of the highest run-getters in T20 cricket, along with compatriot Rohit Sharma, New Zealand's Martin Guptill and Pakistan's Shoaib Malik. But what makes him the best among the others is his average, which is more than 50 – and there's no one close to him.

Most Runs in T20Is

Player	Mat	Inns	Runs	HS	Ave
Rohit Sharma (IND)	94	86	2331	118	32.37
Martin Guptill (NZ)	76	74	2272	105	33.91
Virat Kohli (IND)	**67**	**62**	**2263**	**90***	**50.28**
Shoaib Malik (PAK)	111	104	2263	75	30.58
Brendon McCullum (NZ)	71	70	2140	123	35.66

Mat: Matches; Inns: Innings; HS: Highest score; Ave: Average; xx*: not out

There are only two batsmen in the world with an average of 50-plus in the T20 format. Virat is currently number two on the list.

Highest Averages

Player	Mat	Inns	Runs	HS	Ave
Babar Azam (PAK)	29	29	1182	97*	53.72
Virat Kohli (IND)	**67**	**62**	**2263**	**90***	**50.28**
K.L. Rahul (IND)	27	24	879	110*	43.95
Manish Pandey (IND)	28	23	538	79*	41.38
Michael Hussey (AUS)	38	30	721	60*	37.94

What's more, Virat has been named the Man of the Tournament in the last two T20 World Cups in 2014 and 2016, and he was on the top of the ICC T20 batting rankings for most of the time during the period 2014–17.

In the lead-up to the final of the ICC World T20 in Bangladesh in 2014, Virat scored 242 runs in 5 matches at an average of 121 – which included the innings of 36 not out against Pakistan, 54 against the West Indies,

57 not out against Bangladesh, 23 against Australia, and a match-winning 72 not out against South Africa in the semi-final. Virat was unanimously chosen Man of the Tournament by the group of cricket experts nominated by the ICC.

Then again, in the World T20 in 2016, Virat was instrumental in India's journey to the semi-final and he won the Player of the Tournament award, even though he was disappointed that India did not make it through to the final. He finished as the second highest run-getter of the tournament, with 273 runs in 5 innings, at a breathtaking average of 136.50. He scored three 50s, which included a highest of 89 not out in the semi-final against West Indies, who emerged as eventual champions.

Virat has won the most Man of the Match awards for India in T20Is – ten awards in 67 matches. With two more awards, he will beat the record of Pakistan's Shahid Afridi and Afghanistan's Mohammad Nabi (with eleven each) for most Man of the Match awards in the shortest format.

A different league

India's win in the 2008 Under-19 World Cup under Virat's captaincy happened just a few days before the start of the inaugural edition of IPL. The Royal Challengers of Bangalore (RCB) picked up the nineteen-year-old as a catchment player (under 22 years), bought outside of the IPL auction. He was among the youngest in the team and played most of the matches in that season. It was a great learning experience for him as he shared the dressing room with legends like Chris Gayle, A.B. de Villiers, Daniel Vettori and Anil Kumble.

As far as batting went, the first season was a total failure for him – he scored just 165 runs with an average of 15. The media speculated that he had lost his way among IPL's glamour and riches as well as the momentum he had after the U-19 success. But Virat bounced back stronger and completely changed himself as a person and batsman, becoming more focused on his game.

The RCB owners kept the faith in Virat in the next season too. This time he improved his average from the previous year's 15 to 22.36 and 27.90 in seasons 2009 and 2010. It was still a learning phase for him, but he was a smart and quick student. Even though he scored only two half-centuries in the first three seasons, one could clearly see the spark in him. He was progressing to a different, higher level with each match and each IPL season. He not only matured over the years, he also became far more consistent with his bat.

As his former U-19 coach Lalchand Rajput says, Virat has the gift of great mental toughness. According to Rajput, Virat was never as naturally gifted a batsman as Sachin Tendulkar. Virat worked hard on his batting and with every passing year, he got better and better. The best thing about Virat, Rajput says, is that he gives a 110 per cent. He knows how to play in different situations and when to change gear, when to dominate and when to play safe.

Before the 2011 season, Virat was the only player retained by RCB, and was made the vice-captain under skipper Daniel Vettori. The latter led the team in 2011 and 2012. After Vettori's retirement, Virat was given full-time captaincy and he still leads the team. He has never been auctioned in IPL history. He was acquired by RCB for a nominal price of Rs 20 lakh as part of their U-22 quota and had no international experience whatsoever. In 2019, RCB retained Virat for a whopping Rs 17 crore.

Since the first IPL edition, he is among the few players who has played this format for twelve consecutive seasons for a single team. Under Virat's leadership, RCB made it to the final in 2016, although the winning trophy continues to elude him. He may not have won an IPL trophy for his team, but he has been one of the leading performers with the bat and his statistics tell the story.

Virat's most successful outing in the IPL came in 2016. He slammed 973 runs, the most by any player in *any* T20 tournament in the world. Previously, the highest scores were 733 runs by West Indian cricketer Chris Gayle in the 2012 IPL season and by Michael Hussey in 2013. Virat averaged over 80 with a strike rate of 150, not to forget his four 100s and seven 50s. His four centuries in IPL 2016 set a record for the most by a player in any T20 tournament (the previous highest in the IPL was two centuries by his teammate Chris Gayle in 2011).

Virat bagged the prestigious Orange Cap (presented to the leading run scorer in the IPL) in 2016, where he smashed several illustrious records. The table below shows what happened.

Virat in the IPL – Batting
(Since 2008)

	Mat	Runs	HS	Ave	100s	50s
Career	**163**	**4948**	**113**	**38.35**	**4**	**34**
2018	14	530	92*	48.18	0	4
2017	10	308	64	30.80	0	4
2016	**16**	**973**	**113**	**81.08**	**4**	**7**
2015	16	505	82*	45.90	0	3
2014	14	359	73	27.61	0	2
2013	16	634	99	45.28	0	6

2012	16	364	73*	28.00	0	2
2011	16	557	71	46.41	0	4
2010	16	307	58	27.90	0	1
2009	16	246	50	22.36	0	1
2008	13	165	38	15.00	0	0

Virat became the first player to score 4,000 runs in the IPL during his knock of 113 against Kings XI Punjab. This is also his highest score in the IPL. He has the second-most number of runs in the IPL after Suresh Raina.

Virat was among the runs in IPL season 2018 as well. With 530 runs, he was the highest run scorer for RCB and finished seventh in the overall list. He may well end his career as the best limited-overs batsman ever, and it would be is fair to say that Virat is the best specialist T20 batsman and the biggest T20 match-winner the world has ever seen.

Harbhajan Singh, who too has played ten seasons for Mumbai Indians, says, 'Virat has been a constant contributor over the years. RCB also knows his value – they know he is a match-winner as he gives his more than his 100 per cent. RCB also know that if he goes to auction, he will get three or four times more money than what he is getting right now.'

After his marvellous 82 not out against Australia at Mohali during the World T20 match in 2016, *The*

2016: The Breakthrough Year

Former England Test batsman Mark Butcher keeps Virat on the top of his list and considers him a match-winning player. In an interview to media he said, 'When Virat is on the park … everybody knows that there is a battle on. There is very rarely a dull moment and as captain of India he will get in the opposition's face and won't take a backward step.'[21]

In the year 2016, Virat won many of these battles. The year proved to be the best for Virat's career so far, and that too in all three formats. During these twelve months, he not only led his Test team to series wins against the West Indies, New Zealand and England, he also single-handedly took RCB to the IPL final.

He excelled as the captain in all formats, as batsman in all formats and in the IPL too. He averaged more than 75 in all three international formats and more than 100 in IPL. The closest any player has come to match these records is Kumar Sangakkara in 2013.

Virat widened the gap between himself and other top-order batsmen in the world. In Test matches, he scored 1,215 runs at an average of 75.94 in his 18 innings (his earlier best average was 56 in 2013). He averaged just over 92 in ODIs.

However, the best part was his average in the T20 format. Usually, players have better averages in Tests and ODIs, but in 2016, Virat crossed all limits in this short format – his average crossed 100 in T20Is and more than 80 in IPL. In 2016, Virat scored a total of 641 runs in fifteen T20Is – and again set a record for the most runs scored by a cricketer in T20Is in a year.

Guardian wrote that he had the 'Moxie [force of character, determination, or nerve] of a million men'.[22]

Virat's Dream Run in 2016

Format	Matches	Runs	Average	100s/50s
Tests	12	1215	75.93	4/2
ODIs	10	739	92.37	3/4
T20Is	15	641	106.83	0/7
IPL	16	973	81.08	4/7

There are many discussions in sports circles about the best current batsmen – and they throw up names like Joe Root, Kane Williamson, Steve Smith and A.B. de Villiers. However, none of these batsmen are as dominant across all three cricket formats like Virat is. He is the only cricketer to average 50-plus across all three formats at present. As he is quoted to have said, 'The bat is not a toy, it's a weapon. It gives me everything in life, which helps me to do everything on the field.'[23]

Making the impossible possible on the field is what Virat is all about, and that's what makes him a stellar team player.

Virat is the world's first batsman to score more than 600 runs in a calendar year in T20 internationals. He did it in 2016.

Virat plays a square drive against the West Indies at the Queen's
Park Oval in Port of Spain, Trinidad and Tobago, in 2013

13

The boy who grew into a team player

It was late one night in March 2013. Two cars whizzed past each other on an empty road in Delhi. This is not an uncommon sight in the metropolis; only this time, the drivers were M.S. Dhoni and Virat Kohli. Both ardent Michael Jackson fans, they were rushing to watch a preview show of *This Is It*, a movie tribute to the iconic singer, directed by Kenny Ortega.

This was only one aspect of the camaraderie the two players shared. Their understanding of each other and their rapport helped to build a very strong Indian side. Virat has always respected M.S. Dhoni, especially because of how the latter has led the Indian team.

Dhoni is known to trust young players and groom them to their full potential. And when he had someone like Virat on the team, there were many positive outcomes.

Dhoni wanted the Indian team to be the best fielding side in the world. A natural athlete, Virat was central to this plan. In fact, Virat also admitted that it was their fielding that led the Men in Blue to the final of the Champions Trophy played in England in 2013.

Even when he became captain, Virat never hesitated to seek Dhoni's advice. During an episode of the web series *Breakfast with Champions*, Virat spoke about his faith in Dhoni. He said: 'When running between the wickets and he calls in "two" I just close my eyes and run because his judgement is so correct.'[24]

The cordial relationship that Virat and Dhoni share also has a huge bearing on Indian cricket. A few years after Dhoni suddenly stood down from Test captaincy in 2014, Virat said that he had cried when the announcement was made. Times of transition are not easy for any regime, but Virat filled Dhoni's shoes in the smoothest of ways. This was more evident in ODI as Dhoni was still playing this format. It is also very uncommon to see a captain field at the boundary because they are generally required to stand somewhere close to the bowler and the wicketkeeper to be able to pass on instructions. Not in Virat's case. If the team needed it, he could be found fielding in the far corners of the ground as Dhoni was still around making those small fielding changes whenever required.

Virat and Sachin

'The sandstorm from Sachin at Sharjah and the hailstorm from Virat in Mohali should be written in the same paragraphs,' said Indian spinner R. Ashwin as he saw Virat smash 82 off 51 balls against Australia in the 2016 ICC World T20.[25]

The innings helped India beat Australia and reach the semi-final and Ashwin thought it was comparable to Sachin's legendary Sharjah innings in 1998 when he scored 143 runs off 131 balls to get the team into the final of the tri-series against Australia.

For many, writing about Sachin Tendulkar and Virat Kohli 'in the same paragraph' is sacrilegious. But such has been Virat's performance and impact that every cricket discussion inevitably ends up including a comparison of Sachin and Virat.

Sachin was a young prodigy; he made headlines when he was only sixteen years old. Virat blossomed as a cricketer in his mid-twenties. Sachin was known for his mild manners and soft-spoken nature. Virat, on the other hand, is a flamboyant and aggressive cricketer.

Virat has mentioned many times that he feels embarrassed when he is compared to Sachin and that it is an unfair comparison. But the fact remains that the only player likely to go past Sachin's record of 100 international centuries is Virat, having already achieved two-thirds of this number by March 2019.

When India won the World Cup in 2011, it was Virat who first carried Sachin Tendulkar on his shoulders in front of the spectators and paid tribute to Sachin's twenty-one years of commitment to the country. Sachin, in his autobiography, *Playing It My Way*, mentions the time he had retreated to the Wankhede dressing room, teary-eyed, after he announced his retirement from international cricket. At that time, as a mark of respect, Virat gave Sachin the threads [*mauli* or puja threads] that his own father had given him.

Not only has Virat always shown great respect towards Sachin, he has also carried on his legacy. In 2014, when he had a forgettable series in England, Virat took Sachin's advice. After that, he scored

'...He is going to be one of the leading players in the world, not just of this generation, but one of the leading players of all time'

**SACHIN TENDULKAR,
former Indian cricketer
and captain**

four tons in his next series, in Australia, and maintained his form.

Shane Warne, who once said that he had nightmares about bowling to Sachin, told the press, 'To my mind, what's already evident is that Virat is one of the best players of all time. In one-dayers, he probably has to go down with Viv Richards as the greatest ever, not so much for the record but for the way he plays his game...'[26]

Smells like team spirit

Virat has grown into a perfect team person who respects the senior players and supports the youngsters.

The Indian cricket team is replete with stories of dressing-room heroes. On the ground, cricketers strive to give their best, whether they succeed or not. However, cricket also involves planning, execution, sharing and bonding that mostly happens behind the prying eyes of the press. Cricket tours are long, with the players travelling together for months many times in a year. It is in these times that a person's true character and grit are revealed.

Virat has ensured that the atmosphere in the dressing room is lively and supportive. When the Indian team was embarking on their tour of Australia in 2014, Virat addressed the first team meeting as captain, saying that winning was the most important factor for the team but so was everyone's contribution. He also stressed the importance of enjoying the game and revelling in the successes of other teammates.

While Virat appears to be a no-nonsense leader, he also doesn't miss an opportunity to lift a heavy mood in the changing room. Virat is a natural mimicry artist, and when in the mood, he regales his friends by mimicking artists like Suniel Shetty and Anil Kapoor, among others. In fact, during the break in a match in 2016, a DJ was playing an Anil Kapoor song and Virat was fielding near the boundary. When Virat heard the song, he broke into an impromptu jig, to loud cheers from the crowd. When relaxing after tough training sessions, Virat likes to listen to Punjabi songs. He is a fan of Sukhbir and knows most of his numbers by heart. Coach Rajkumar says, 'He loves Punjabi songs and also hums whenever he gets a chance.'

However, Virat is no longer light-hearted when it comes to another aspect of his life!

In 2018, Virat became the fastest captain to reach 8,000 runs in international cricket. He achieved this feat in a match against West Indies in Visakhapatnam, Andhra Pradesh.

14

The boy who became a fitness icon

Gone are the days when player's talent and capability were the only parameters for securing a berth on a national cricket team. Fitness is a very important aspect in any sport these days for a player to perform well and continue to do that for longer!

In this new era of sport, players and management have aligned themselves for total fitness. Indian sportspersons these days, following a strict diet plan and sweating it out in the gym, are now considered among the in-shape players in the world. And leading this pack in the world is India's cricket captain.

Not only has Virat achieved a high level of fitness, he has also set an example for others in the team. The current Indian cricket team under Captain Kohli is by far the fittest in its history. Virat feels that an unfit body is an invitation to negativity.

Managing time to perfection and keeping oneself mentally and physically fit to be consistent in all formats of the game is his new mantra of life, irrespective of the game situation. 'For me, it is not winning one Test match and saying we made history and then not being able to follow that up,' he said in an interview with *The Telegraph*. 'I want us to be the fittest Indian team that has played the game as well.'[27]

Fitness and fielding

Let's look back at the fitness of Indian cricket players in the 1980s and 1990s.

In his column for the *Mumbai Mirror*, Suresh Menon, one of India's most experienced cricket writers, describes fielding, 'In the early days of Indian cricket, the Maharajahs thought nothing of actually having their servants fielding for them,' he wrote. '…it allowed the batsmen to have a prolonged rest, and the bowlers to come off the field after every spell.'[28] Not even a Test captain – the Maharajkumar of Vizianagaram – was above this.

From the 1950s to the 70s, India had wonderfully gifted batsmen and bowlers, but it was hard to find a great fielder. The Indian side of the 1970s had just one such player – an outstandingly close catcher called Eknath Solkar, arguably the greatest short-leg fielder in the history of the game, fielding without a helmet and even without shin guards. (*Short leg*, also known as *bat pad*, is a cricket fielding position specifically intended to catch balls that unintentionally strike the bat and leg pad, and end up only a metre or two to the leg side.) In contrast, West Indian greats Clive Lloyd and Vivian Richards spoke several times about how the 1970s world champions, the West Indians, achieved supremacy because of their fitness. It was not the same with Indian cricket back then.

Earlier generations of Indian cricketers did not have proper trainers to guide them with fielding drills and warm-ups. Players managed their fitness routines more or less on their own. Besides, the grounds were uneven and grassless in those days, causing many of the cricketers to develop a dislike for fielding.

The great former Indian captain Mansoor Ali Khan Pataudi said in an interview with Karan Thapar in *Devil's Advocate* on CNN IBN: 'Throughout the history of Indian cricket, fielding has been very poor. We don't have the grounds to learn fielding. We don't know how to dive; we don't know how to slide because we don't have such ground... we can slide on.'[29] However, in the 1980s, Kapil Dev stood out as a fine outfielder as well as an agile one in the slips. Who can forget his catch of Vivian

Richards off Madan Lal's ball, which turned the 1983 World Cup final in India's favour! But, except a few, the Indian team was marked as a poor bunch of fielders. Many of them were unfit and overweight.

In the 1990s, Indian cricket saw brilliant fielders in Mohammad Azharuddin, Robin Singh and Ajay Jadeja. But fielding was not given as much importance as batting or bowling until South African Jonty Rhodes came into the cricketing world. Rhodes is one of those players in cricket history who are better known for their fielding than their batting. This was the first time India started focusing on its fielding abilities.

Since then, our grounds have improved, coaches have begun to focus on fielding and budding players know that better fielding will help them move ahead of competitors. In the mid-1990s and 2000s, the Indian team had brilliant fielders such as Yuvraj Singh, Suresh Raina, Shikhar Dhawan and Mohammad Kaif, who never thought twice about diving and saved a lot of runs whenever they played.

The age of Virat

Virat's fitness is a story in itself. He was not always like this. When he came on to the scene in late 2008, he was a chubby lad. During his early career on the international platform, he did not take fitness seriously.

So how did he transform himself from a fat-cheeked boy to a fitness icon, bringing an in-shape culture into the team? Former Australian Captain Michael Clarke says, 'Virat takes fitness as seriously as his batting and fielding. That's one thing Virat has certainly enforced on this Indian team. He wants everybody strong and fitter, to prevent injuries – to be able to be successful for a long period of time – to sustain till day four and day five of the Test matches. So he is spending a lot of time in the gym and also focusing on his diet.'

The transformation began in 2012, when after showing poor form in the IPL, Virat realized the importance of staying fit. He started taking it seriously, and changed his training patterns and eating habits completely.

In an interview with PTI, Virat explained his story, 'It changed in 2012. I had great tours to Australia and scored 180 against Bangladesh and went into the IPL thinking: "Wow, this is going to be a great season for me." I wanted to make it my tournament and dominate the bowlers. I really struggled.'[30]

Virat changed his routine when the former coach of the Indian team, former Zimbabwean cricketer Duncan Fletcher, made a life-changing suggestion. Virat recounted his advice in an interview to Michael Vaughan in *The Telegraph* (UK): 'Duncan told me once that he feels cricket is the most unprofessional of professional sports.

You can have the skill but do not think you need to train as much as a tennis player. But I realized if you want to stay longer on top playing three formats, you need a set pattern of your training, the way you eat, how healthy and fit you need to be. Being fitter made me mentally stronger. It was like a direct connection.'[31]

Immediately after this, Virat went off gluten, wheat, cold drinks, and desserts. For the first few months, it was not easy because he loved food. 'I wanted to eat the bed sheet when I went to sleep because I was so hungry,' he said. 'I was craving taste. I was craving delicious food. But then I saw the results. I felt quick around the field. I would wake up in morning and feel like I had energy.'[32]

Not only did he change his diet, but on the advice of the Indian cricket team's strength and conditioning coach, Shankar Basu, he also took up weightlifting. 'Basu introduced me to weightlifting, and that has made me realize what actually one needs to do … I don't do upper body. I only work on my legs for explosive power. He makes me do a crazy number of squats, close to a 100 in a session,' Virat said in a media interaction.[33]

His former teammate Ashish Nehra points out, 'After 2011–12, Virat changed his lifestyle. He shifted gear – between 2012–13 and 2014–15, and 2016, you will see the changes on his face. He has added fitness and that has reflected in his batting as well. He has great intensity and once he pledges something, he completes it with perfection.'

From 2015 onwards, Virat changed his training again under the supervision of Shankar Basu. 'It was unbelievable. I saw the result. I remember running after a ball in a Test series in Sri Lanka and I felt more power in my legs. It was, like "wow". This training is addictive. It has taken my game to another level,' he said to the press.[34]

His childhood coach is a happy man to see Virat's success as a player, as captain and as the team's fitness motivator. 'If you see his knocks across all formats, it tells a story about his fitness,' says Coach Sharma. 'He balances his time and spends as much time working on his cricketing skills as he does on improving his fitness.'

Virat is compared to the football icon Cristiano Ronaldo and the tennis great Rafael Nadal in terms of fitness, and Virat is a fan of both these sportsmen. Just as he redefined his cricket after a slump in form in the early part of his career, Virat made it a point that his high fitness levels would push his cricket to the next stage. He is now one of the biggest influencers of the fitness industry, creating awareness among the youth to help them lead a healthy and fit lifestyle.

Virat, who was not the quickest of fielders earlier, nor willing to field in every position, became fitter, lighter, and stronger, and it soon became second nature to him. High fitness levels have become an integral part of cricket in India as the selection of a player into the team now depends on a certain level of fitness. Credit should be given to Virat leading this fitness regimen in the team and implementing the Yo-Yo Test (*see box below*). In August 2017, a few months after he was handed the captaincy across all formats, Virat had a talk with the team management and this test was made mandatory for each player to retain his place in the national team. The current Indian cricketers have taken fielding to a whole new level.

The Yo-Yo Test

Danish scientist Dr Jens Bangsbo created this test in the 1990s to evaluate a football player's aerobic endurance and fitness. It was later adopted by other sports. Unlike football or tennis, which require continuous running or movement, cricket it is a start-stop sport. A player is physically active in periods (running between the wickets or bowling) and gets time to recover in the middle as well (while fielding

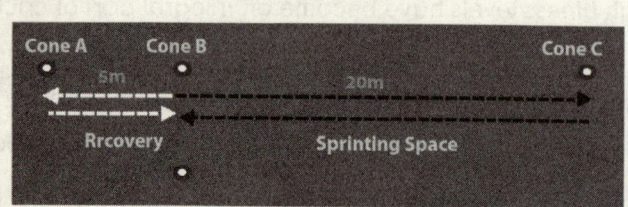

or when waiting to bat). The test helps players recover faster and better during matches by increasing their aerobic ability.

Three cones, say A, B and C, are placed on a flat surface in a straight line. The distance between cone B and C is 20 km and distance between cone A and B is 5 km. The player runs from cone B to C and then back from C to B. Once the player reaches B, they get a 10-second rest period where they run from cone B to A and back to B. This is one 'shuttle'.

As the level goes up, the time for completing the shuttle decreases. Speed level 5, the starting level, has one shuttle; speed level 9, the next one, also has one. Level 11 has two, level 12 has three, level 13 has 4, and so on. The total distance covered is their official score, measured on a software.

Vegan vibes

Once there was a boy who loved butter chicken, biryani and kebabs, then in mid-2018, he suddenly turned vegan, joining tennis champion Serena Williams and football star Lionel Messi. A self-confessed foodie, Virat gave up animal protein and dairy products, and replaced them with protein shakes, vegetables and soy in his regular diet.

As he entered his thirties, Virat said he had adopted a vegan diet to extend the quality of cricket he was playing. Talking to the media during a press conference, he said, 'I want to be able to play this kind of cricket even when I am thirty-four or thirty-five. You know, that's why I train so much because I am a guy who likes to play with intensity. Once that is gone, I don't know what I am gonna do on the field.'[35]

'We have seen Sachin Tendulkar as a role model for his focus on fitness, but Virat took it to a different level,' Harbhajan Singh says. 'We can say that he made fitness a compulsory thing in Indian cricket. He broke with tradition by making fitness key for selection [to the national squads]. He showed that fitness not only improves fielding standards but can also raise your game. He set a benchmark and has become a terrific role model for the next generation.'

In 2017, Virat appeared on the TV show *Breakfast with Champions* hosted by Gaurav Kapur and talked about his diet plan in detail. He revealed that he hadn't had his favourite butter chicken and naan in four years![36]

Virat's Fitness Mantras

- Virat works out for at least two hours, five days a week. So, exercise daily, no matter what, with a focus on building your stamina and body strength, rather than losing weight.
- Home-cooked food is the best because it doesn't have harmful preservatives. He does not believe in eating less to stay healthy. Rather, he believes in eating as much as his body can easily digest.
- Avoid junk food wherever possible.
- Virat follows his diet strictly, but he has a cheat day occasionally. (A cheat day usually means having small quantities of whatever you crave and enjoying it slowly.)
- He eats a light dinner with soups and salads as the best options. 'During game time, he has protein shakes with carbs from good sources.
- Virat completely avoids smoking and alcohol.

Featuring on the cover of the Guide to Style section of *Men's Health* magazine in 2012, he had said that whoever wants to stay fit should follow the 'eat, sleep, train, repeat' pattern. 'A fit body gives you confidence,' he said. And there's nothing more impressive than a great attitude, which you can wear on your sleeve.'[37]

As Virat said to the media, 'It started off as something that is required for my sport, but now it is a lifestyle choice for me. Even when I don't play or even during my off time I don't eat unhealthy food.'[38] He also sometimes put up posts of his cardio session or his fit body on social media.

Today, fitness is key to any team's success at the international level. Michael Clarke, while talking about the fitness, says, 'Virat has brought in some really strict discipline and routines around the food that the Indian team is consuming.'

As with fitness, Virat has set some serious goals as the most wanted candidate for product and endorsements, making Brand Virat Kohli a popular proposition.

Virat's Body Statistics*

Height	5'9"
Weight:	69 kg
Chest:	42 in
Arms/Biceps:	15 in
Waist:	31 in

* Approximately

The Fitness Challenge –
#HumFitTohIndiaFit

To promote the benefits of exercise and workout, India's sports minister Rajyavardhan Singh Rathore kick-started a Fitness Challenge drive on social media in May 2015, called #HumFitTohIndiaFit. He urged Indians to shoot a video of their 'fitness mantra' and share it on Twitter. He challenged Virat and few other stars to take it forward.

Virat responded with his fitness video and challenged Indian Prime Minister Narendra Modi, star cricketer M.S. Dhoni, and his wife and actor Anushka Sharma to match it. 'Challenge accepted, Virat,' the prime minister wrote in his response to the cricketer's tweet.

Virat took just 10 years and 68 days to score 10,000 ODI runs, the fastest by a batsman. He broke Rahul Dravid's record of 10 years and 317 days.

15

The boy who evolved into a celebrity brand

Cricket is a national passion and an obsession with millions of followers and fans. Not only does it catapult its heroes to a high pedestal, it is also a lucrative sport nowadays, especially with the rise of the IPL. Cricketers who make it to the top earn lots of money through match fees as well as sponsorship and endorsement deals with the largest brands in India and the world.

Virat symbolizes the spirit of youth today. His growing maturity over the years, his consistency in batting and his leadership abilities as India's cricket captain have turned the spotlight on him, and it follows him everywhere. He is captain, rebel, match-winner and achiever all rolled into one – and appeals to everyone in the house.

He not only leads from the front, but also takes responsibility for the losses. With his attitude, honesty and personality on and off the field, he is now considered to the top choice for brands to engage and attract consumers. He can be found everywhere on TV advertisements, brand endorsements and digital media platforms. From the airport to railway stations, from posh markets to local bazaars, you will see Virat on hoardings and posters, representing the biggest brands all across the country. As a brand, he is omnipresent.

The best batsman in world cricket is on a mission to break several records written in the history of the game. It seems only a matter of time till he surpasses Sachin Tendulkar's record of forty-nine centuries in ODIs. And he could very well go past the Master Blaster's untouchable 'hundred hundreds' at some stage in his career. In his ten years in international cricket, Virat has evolved into a credible and trusty personality whom top national and international brands want to sign as the face of their products and services.

In the 1990s and early 2000s, it was Bollywood that dominated brand endorsements. Athletes were never really considered before David Beckham changed the game internationally. In India too perceptions changed, and cricket stars such as Sachin Tendulkar, Sourav Ganguly and M.S. Dhoni were soon found endorsing as many brands as film stars. Sachin ruled the market and was at the forefront for almost a decade. He owned close to 80 per cent of the sports market in India, and reigned supreme till the mid-2000s, until M.S. Dhoni came to town.

Dhoni's remarkable on-field success led to his incredible off-field brand value. But neither Sachin nor Dhoni achieved the scale Virat has garnered on the commercial pitch, displacing not only top cricketers but Bollywood stars too.

From boy to super-brand

Virat made his debut in 2008 and by the mid 2010s, the youth of the nation wanted to be like him. Everything from his aggressive on-field demeanour to his fashion sense, hairstyle and tattoos were picked up by the young and the bold. Even cricketers from neighbouring countries began to emulate Virat's style.

Virat's Tattoos

Virat has got himself inked several times, as far as public knowledge goes. Here's a list of his tattoos, each a meaningful one, according to him.

#1: *Prem and Saroj*: (left arm) The names of his parents.

#2: *A monastery*: (left forearm) It symbolizes peace of mind and its power.

#3: *Samurai*: (left upper arm) It symbolizes his fight to achieve what he has and master self-discipline. The seven virtues a Japanese warrior practises are: Gi (justice), Yu (courage), Jin (benevolence), Rei (politeness), Makoto (honesty), Meiyo (honor) and Chugi (loyalty).

#4: *Lord Shiva*: (left arm below elbow) Against the background of Mount Kailash and Lake Mansarovar, the Hindu god Shiva is the Destroyer of Evil and the God of creation.

#5: *God's eye*: (on his left shoulder) The all-seeing eye that keeps track of everything one does. It also stands for intuition.

#6: *175 and 269*: (left upper arm) In 2008, Virat made his ODI debut against Sri Lanka in Dambulla and became the 175th Indian cricketer to play for India in ODIs. Three years later, he became the 269th Indian to represent India in Test matches.

#7: *Tribal art symbol*: One of the first tattoos he got; it is said to represent positive aggression.

#8: *Scorpio*: (right bicep) Virat's zodiac sign.

#9: *Om*: (next to the all-seeing eye) The universal sound; the essence of life.

Virat is managed by Cornerstone Sport and Entertainment, whose founder Bunty Sajdeh spotted him during the 2008 Under-19 World Cup and signed him up before he became a regular for India. Virat is said to endorse brands he relates to. In an interview in *Mint*, Sajdeh said, 'He does not mince his words ever. This is something the young of today admire and appreciate. He wears his heart on his sleeve and is never afraid to call a spade a spade.'[39]

Brand Kohli has been steadily on the rise after the T20 event in 2012. His on-field performance, especially his innings against Pakistan, and his best knocks during tough chases, catapulted him into stardom. In the same year, Virat featured among *GQ* magazine's top ten best-dressed men worldwide. The list included the likes of actor Michael Fassbender, Canadian actor and musician Ryan Gosling, and former US President Barack Obama. This was the time when global fashion and apparel companies were aggressively promoting themselves in India. Virat, along with Anjana Reddy's Universal Sportsbiz, launched his own apparel brand, Wrogn, which caters to urban youth.

After a fabulous 2016, the king of cricket dethroned the king of Bollywood, Shah Rukh Khan, in December 2017 to become the most valuable celebrity brand in the country. Virat registered a growth of 56 per cent over the previous year and was valued at US$144 million (around Rs 990 crore). It was an astonishing achievement, because Shah Rukh Khan had redefined the meaning of a 'brand' since the turn of the century.

The Indian captain is one of the best-paid athletes in the world and is the only Indian to be included in the *Forbes* list of the highest paid athletes of 2017 and 2018. According to TAM Media Research, in 2016–17, Virat's per day exposure was at 196 minutes across all television channels, promoting brands such as Colgate, TVS, Vicks, Clear Shampoo, Pepsi, Audi, Britannia, Lloyd and MRF.[40] More importantly, in 82 per cent of these advertisements, Virat was the solo star, which is a testament to the player's popularity and bankability.

Look at his list of brand-value achievements below:

- **ESPN World Fame 100:** This list placed Indian cricket team captain Virat Kohli at the seventh position and he is the only Indian athlete in the top ten. This evaluation includes the Portuguese footballer Cristiano Ronaldo at the top spot, followed by basketball player LeBron James and FC Barcelona captain Lionel Messi. Virat is just above the number eight Rafael Nadal, while Dhoni is placed at the thirteenth spot.[41]

- **Forbes India Celebrity 100:** The Indian cricket captain is the first sportsperson to make it to the second spot in this list, right behind Bollywood superstar Salman Khan. This evaluation has traditionally been dominated by showbiz personalities. Besides Akshay Kumar, Deepika Padukone, Aamir Khan, Ranveer Singh and Ajay Devgn, it includes Dhoni at fifth spot and Tendulkar at ninth. According to *Forbes*, the world's highest-paid cricketer's brand value is at US$14.5 million (approximately Rs 105 crore), which is higher than that of football icon Lionel Messi, golf superstar Rory McIlroy, and Golden State Warriors' Stephen Curry.[42]

- **Duff & Phelps – Celebrity Brand Valuation Report 2018:** This report provides a ranking of India's most powerful celebrity brands based on brand values derived from their endorsement contracts. The fourth edition of this report, titled 'The Bold, the Beautiful and the Brilliant', was announced in 2018. Virat retained the top position for the second consecutive year. His brand value rose by 18 per cent to US$170.9 million (around 1,168 crore) in 2018. Deepika Padukone rose to the second position, whereas Shah Rukh Khan fell to fifth position.[43]

Brand expert Harish Bijoor of Harish Bijoor Consults Inc., a private-label consulting firm that specializes in brand and business strategy, says, 'Cricket today harvests the primary emotion of the nation, and that is a valuable item for brands to harvest in turn. Virat the brand has the potential, thanks to his savvy looks, his in-the-face attitude, and most certainly, his status as a part of the celebrity-couple brigade, to crack into the international brand endorsement league. If any cricketer in the history of Indian cricket has a chance to enter here and dominate, it is Virat.... he is the reigning lord of the brand-endorsement world.'

The cricketer currently endorses around twenty-five brands such as Audi, Manyavar, Puma, Wrogn, Tissot, Boost Energy, MuveAcoustics, MRF Tyres, Gionee, Colgate, Hero MotoCorp, American Tourister, Philips India, Sun Pharma, Vicks India, Royal Challenge Sports Drink, Remit2India and Valvoline India. His new deals include e-commerce firm Flipkart, health-snack brand Too Yum and online taxi app Uber. In 2017, he ended his association with Pepsi, indicating that he would only endorse brands with a pro-health image.

Business as usual

A sportsperson's life as a player can be short and Virat has several enterprises off the field.

2014

- Football is said to be Virat's second favourite sport. In 2014, he bought the FC Goa franchise of the Indian Super League (ISL) because as a football lover he wanted to see the sport grow in India.
- He became the brand ambassador for and a stakeholder in the London-based social networking venture, Sport Convo.
- Virat, in association with Anjana Reddy's Universal Sportsbiz (USPL), launched a fashion label Wrogn. The brand sells men's casual wear and has tied up with major online e-commerce companies.

2015

- Virat became the co-owner of the UAE Royals franchise of the International Premier Tennis League (IPTL). The IPTL is an annual team tennis event that is played across various cities in Asia.
- He invested a total of Rs 90 crore in a chain of gyms and fitness centres called Chisel. Virat co-owns the fitness chain jointly with Chisel India and Cornerstone Sport and Entertainment.

- Virat became a co-owner of the Bengaluru Yodhas franchise of the Indian Pro Wrestling League, along with the JSW group.
- In association with Stepathlon Lifestyle, Virat launched Stepathlon Kids – a fitness venture for children.

Virat is currently the highest paid player in the IPL. His phenomenal rise is expected to make him the richest cricketer of all time by the time he hangs up his boots. His ability to reap the whirlwind not only in India, but also across the Indian cricket diaspora markets of the world, makes him the biggest individual brand in the country.

Experts believe that if Virat continues on his path, Brand Kohli could see an even greater upsurge in commercial engagements and his valuation.

 Virat has the most 200-plus scores by a Test captain anywhere in the world, totalling six.

One of Virat's many brand endorsements

16

The boy who met a girl

India is a country where cricket and Bollywood, two professions in the limelight, have always had a connection, and it can be traced back decades.

Way back in the 1960s, Hindi cinema star Sharmila Tagore and the youngest and most successful Test captain of India (also the Nawab of Pataudi), Mansoor Ali Khan Pataudi, tied the knot. The country has seen many such pairs, with the latest being that of Virat Kohli and Anushka Sharma.

He is the poster boy of the cricket world and she is one of the finest Bollywood actors and producers. Together, they make a couple adored and followed by many fans, and their wedding was a highlight of 2017. Their relationship continues to be in the limelight.

Bowled over

It is believed that Virat and Anushka first met while shooting for a TV commercial in 2013. By this time, Anushka had earned a nomination for the Filmfare Best Actress award for *Rab Ne Bana Di Jodi* (2008), and critical acclaim for *Band Baaja Baaraat* (2010) and *Jab Tak Hai Jaan* (2012) – which won her Fimfare's Best Supporting Female Actress award. Virat and Anushka hit it off right from the start. Rumours about their relationship began doing the rounds after media and fans spotted them together in India and elsewhere in 2014.

Anushka was often seen cheering the cricket superstar from the VIP gallery during international and IPL matches. They also made it kind of official by attending events together and visiting each other at work. They made their first public appearance together in October 2014, where the two went to watch an Indian Super League (ISL) game together (Virat co-owns an ISL team: FC Goa). And when Virat blew a kiss with his bat to his lady love after scoring a half-century against Sri Lanka in Hyderabad in November 2014, it made headlines.

Soon they both spoke about being in a relationship and made their first official red carpet appearance together at the Vogue Beauty Awards in Mumbai in July 2015.

The outside edge

Like many celebrities in relationships that are always in the public eye, Virat and Anushka too faced their share of controversies and problems. The worst was when Anushka received a backlash whenever Virat failed to perform on field. Strangely enough, she was blamed for India's defeat or Virat's below-par showing – be it during her visit to England in 2014 or the ICC World Cup 2015 semi-final against Australia in Sydney.

During the promotion of *NH10* in the year 2015, Anushka lost her cool as she was being unfairly grilled on her relationship with Virat. Some time later, Virat abused a journalist after a practice session, confusing him with some other journalist who had written a story on him and Anushka in a leading daily. Virat later apologized to him.

Then, news of Anushka and Virat's break-up cropped up in early 2016. There are several stories about the reason, but both of them maintained a silence over it.

Now when Virat performed well, people put up offending memes and posts about Anushka. There were comments thanking her 'for breaking up with Virat'. While the actor chose to mostly remain mum on the issue, it was Virat who came out in full support of her and slammed those who blamed her for his or Indian team's failure. In a long post on Twitter, Virat said: *'Shame on those people who have been having a go at Anushka for the longest time and connecting every negative thing to her … Shame on blaming and making fun of her when she has no control over what I do with my sport. If anything she has only motivated and given me more positivity…'*

High-scoring partnership

Soon, just a few months later, the fans of the couple had something to be happy about as two sorted out their differences and 'Virushka' were back together again. They surprised everyone when they came together to attend the success party of *Sultan* (in which Anushka was the female lead) at Salman Khan's residence. Virat went on to thank Anushka several times for making him a better person.

Rumours of their engagement were in the air and they made more than a handful of public appearances together.

The perfect match

When Virat informed the BCCI in October 2017 that he wanted to skip the ODI and T20 leg of the home series against Sri Lanka, it was clear that a wedding was around the corner. Virat and Anushka finally tied the knot on 11 December 2017 at Borgo Finocchieto, a countryside luxury resort in Tuscany, Italy. It was an intimate wedding attended by their close family and friends.

The two shared photographs on their social media channels with a message, reading: 'Today we have promised each other to be bound in love forever. We are truly blessed to share the news with you. This beautiful day will be made more special with the love and support of our family of fans and well-wishers. Thank you for being such an important part of our journey.' 'Virushka' was trending on social media for more than 24 hours. Their wedding reception in Delhi was attended by Prime Minister Narendra Modi.

In just about a year and a bit more, Virat was going to blaze a new trail in cricket.

 Virat is third on the list of all-time top scorers in overseas Tests in any calendar year.

17

The boy who made cricket history

After taking on the captaincy from M.S. Dhoni in the Test format, Virat started dreaming of winning a series overseas, especially in nations like South Africa, England, New Zealand and Australia – known now as the 'SENA' countries. Being part of the team since 2008, Virat always did his best to help the team win matches abroad. Team India had performed well under previous captains but winning a Test series in Australia and South Africa was still a dream.

Skipper Kohli, who has always focused on making his team the best travelling side, had four series lined up in 2018, and that too against the SENA countries. The team were to play eleven Tests away from home, where they would be tested on every front.

True tests of grit

The year 2018 started with a difficult tour. India were playing three Test matches, a six-match ODI series, and three T20Is. Winning this contest in South Africa, after a four-year gap, was not going to be an easy task, considering how dominant the South Africans had always been in their backyard.

The Indian broadcaster Sony TV's sports wing launched a campaign titled *'Hisaab 25 Saal Ka'* (payback for twenty-five years) stressing that India had not won a Test series in South Africa since their first tour in 1992.

Virat was in top form in 2017 – he had broken many records and was on the verge of surpassing many more. But the pressure was on him both as captain and batsman. After winning nine Test series in a row, Virat's team was ready for the real 'test'. Not only that, the team's number one status at Test cricket was also at stake.

Touted as the most competent team to defeat the home team, Virat's army was seriously challenged. Their winning streak came to a halt as the Indian camp lost the first two Tests. The batting line-up failed miserably, except for Virat's mesmerizing 153 runs off 217 balls in the second Test match.

As they were on the verge of series whitewash, Virat was visibly unhappy with the team's performance. He was also upset with the match officials because a few of their decisions had cost the team heavily. However, one of his good qualities is that he doesn't live in the past. As he said to PTI in May 2016, 'Every day is a new day, every series is a new series. I always feel that there is a scope for improvement, and with every game, I take the plus and the minus as this helps me improvise. There is no substitute to hard work and discipline.'[44]

The Indian team arrived in Johannesburg with new vigour and resolution. Virat made the right call at the toss. Batting first, India set a target of 241 before the home team. South Africa were 124 for 1 wicket and they were looking all set to win the match until just before tea break. What followed was typical cricket lore – the Indian pace attack spearheaded a dramatic collapse of the South African team, which folded at 177 and India won by 63 runs on the fourth day of the final Test.

Muhammad Ali, American former heavyweight champion boxer and one of the greatest sporting figures of the twentieth century, once said, 'The man who has no imagination has no wings.' Imagination is all about seeing the possibilities of doing great things. It lights a fire within us. In an interview to the media, Virat too talked about the power of imagination: '...[in the Johannesburg Test] Dale was bowling a few bouncers when I was in my thirties. He kept urging me to pull. Then I saw that one ball for which I had visualized a proper pull shot, playing it down, and I beat deep square leg four feet to his left. I hit it that hard. So I felt: this is exactly what I had imagined and this is exactly what happened.'[45]

The win at Johannesburg is one of Indian cricket's most famous wins. Besides the bowlers' performance, Virat's two spectacular innings on an extremely tough pitch were crucial in this historical win. With 286 runs in the three Tests, Virat was the most successful batsman in the series.

Vivian Richards, the West Indian great, explains Virat's consistent success. 'We know he has got magnificent skills,' Richards says, 'but the thing that impresses me more than anything else is his seriousness about the

> 'He is always judging the right time to consolidate and the right time to seize a game by the scruff of the neck.'
>
> **A.B. DE VILLIERS, South African international cricketer**

game and his will. You can see that is why he is so successful. A lot of other cricketers with great talent lack that.' Virat was proving him right.

This last match of the series also tested Virat's skills as captain. The critics who were not impressed with his captaincy in the first two Tests saw some great fielding placements and bowling changes. Virat felt that India could have won the series had it been a five-match tournament. Though it lost the series 2–1, the Indian team had struck a triumphant note at the end. The momentum now swung in its favour before the limited overs cricket.

Led by Virat, the Indian cricket team created history by winning the first *ever* bilateral ODI series in South Africa. (India had never won an ODI series here since India's first tour of the country in 1992!) Such was Virat's dominance in this epic series that Shikhar Dhawan, who was the second highest run scorer, followed with only 200 runs, behind Virat's whopping total of 558 runs. Virat scored more runs than South African batsmen Faf du Plessis, Hashim Amla, A.B. de Villiers, Aiden Markram and David Miller combined! For his brilliant form in the series, Virat was adjudged Man of the Match and Man of the Series. Virat also became the first Indian batsman to score three centuries in a bilateral series. With these 500-plus runs, he set a new record for most runs in a bilateral ODI series. The record was previously held by his teammate Rohit Sharma, who scored 491 runs in a six-match series against Australia.

It was one of the most successful overseas wins in Indian cricket history. Team India retained their world number one ranking in Tests and also reclaimed the same in ODIs.

Fighting one's demons

India were still looking for a landmark away series win. And England was next. This time the host broadcaster Sony Six promoted the series as #KyaHogaIssBaar (What will happen this time?).

India had been beaten 4–0 in Tests in 2011 and had also lost the 2014 Test series in England. They needed to prove their dominance in Test cricket, and Virat and coach Ravi Shastri had their sights trained on this series. India were not just the ICC world number one team, they were also the best side to visit England since South Africa had been there under captain Graeme Smith in 2012.

For Virat, as a batsman, the last England tour in 2014 had been a nightmare as the swinging ball had tormented him left, right and centre. He averaged just around 13 in that series, nicking off outside the off stump six times out of ten. His failure against bowler James 'Jimmy'

Anderson and company forced him to rethink his entire technique. After the debacle, Virat had requested his childhood inspiration, the legendary Sachin Tendulkar, to help correct his batting.

The former India coach Lalchand Rajput says, 'He [Virat] called me, came to the Mumbai Cricket Association's indoor facility and had an intense session, and Sachin was present too. Virat worked on his off-stump game. His hard work to correct his game made me his fan that day.' It is this sort of meticulous attention to detail that makes Virat one of the world's greatest athletes.

Having won 2–1 in the T20I series preceding the Tests, he could not stop England from levelling the honours with a 2–1 victory in ODI series.

Virat's ghosts of his last tour in England were buried when he scored 149 and 51 in the first Test at Edgbaston, but it was for a losing cause. India were beaten, and at the second Test at Lord's, suffered an embarrassing 159-run innings defeat. '…Not proud of the way we've played…We deserved to lose this game,' Virat said.[46]

Team India made a comeback in the third Test and England were all out for 317, well short of the mammoth victory target of 521 runs. It was a complete team performance ably led by the skipper himself – he was the best batsman across both sides, after knocks of 97 and 103 in the third Test. 'This was one country where he wanted to score runs, and he worked hard and it really paid off,' says Harbhajan Singh.

When Virat led the team in 2018 in England, he had a sensational run with the bat in the Test series. In five Tests, he scored 593 runs, which included two centuries at an average of 59.30, finishing the series as the highest run-getter. The best part was that he also managed to not get out to Jimmy Anderson even once in the series.

Virat had now scored hundreds against all SENA countries. He showed his class and won the battle against his long-time nemesis, Anderson. Virat was named Man of the Match, and he dedicated the win and the award to those suffering from the floods in Kerala at the time.

In the end, India lost the next two Test matches and result was 4–1 in favour of England. Even though he had impressed everyone with his batting, experts felt that Virat had failed as a captain. With two hundreds and three half-centuries, Virat scored 593 runs in the series and this is how he measured against other visiting captains in England:

Most Runs by a Visiting Captain in a Test Series in England

Captain	Matches	Runs	Year
Gary Sobers (WI)	5	722	1966
Graeme Smith (SA)	5	714	2003
Allan Border(AUS)	6	597	1985

Virat Kohli (IND)	**5**	**593**	**2018**
Alan Melville (SA)	5	544	1947

During the series, Virat also completed 4,000 runs as Test captain, becoming the first Indian to do so. He was also the fastest to reach the landmark, in just 63 innings in 38 Test matches, surpassing Brian Lara.

Fastest to 4,000 Runs as Test Captain

Batsman	Team	Matches	Innings
Virat Kohli	**India**	**39**	**45**
Brian Lara	West Indies	40	71
Ricky Ponting	Australia	42	75
Greg Chappell	Australia	45	80
Allan Border	Australia	49	83

Whether it was the hard deck at the Centurion or the seaming conditions of Birmingham and Nottingham, which helped bowlers get movement off the pitch, Virat's dazzling stroke play kept the fans hooked to the game. On the personal front, the tour of England and the 593 runs in the Test series reaffirmed his status as a present-day cricketing great. Even his critics stood up and applauded as Virat let his bat do all the talking. The tour of England put the full stop on the debate about the best batsman in the world in the modern era.

A historic haul

To win the series that India were to play in Australia, the Border–Gavaskar Trophy, remained a dream for India. Ahead of the much-anticipated India's tour Down Under, the host broadcaster Sony Ten3 chose the tagline #Chhodnamat (Don't leave them!) – which highlighted the team's attitude.

Australian cricket had just seen the downfall of two of their main players, captain Steve Smith and vice-captain David Warner, after the Sandpaper Crisis – a ball tampering scandal. In short, Australian batsman Cameron Bancroft, during a Test match in Cape Town, used sandpaper smuggled to the field to rough up the ball in an attempt to help his bowlers. Smith and Warner were given year-long bans from all international and domestic cricket, and Bancroft was suspended for nine months. The Australian team suffered eight defeats in their last nine series in all formats and it gave India a better chance to win their first series Down Under in 70 years, under Virat's leadership.

Former Australian international cricketer and currently coach and commentator Michael Hussey, famously known as 'Mr Cricket', said before the series, 'Lots of

Australian fans – they love Virat because they could see a bit of Australian in him. He is an amazing player in all formats of the game … I just love his competitiveness: he is aggressive, he is uncompromising, he plays a tough, hard brand of cricket and his passion to win every game is fantastic. It can be a big series for him if India win this.'[47]

The former Australia captain Allan Border, after whom the series is named, thinks Virat is the face of new India. 'He is an exceptional young man and a player with lots of character,' says Border.

The pressure was on this young man who had lost two overseas series in 2018. 'We're not taking anything for granted,' Virat said at the press conference before the series. '…We're looking to correct things that haven't gone right in the past.'[48]

After a year of trying to win on foreign soil, the Indian caravan reached Adelaide, burdened with a history of loss. Besides,

'Virat's consistency with the bat is beyond phenomenal… he learns from his mistakes and to then avoid those.'

SUNIL GAVASKAR,
former Indian
international cricketer
and captain

they were hard pressed to maintain their number one Test status.

India's warm-up match in Sydney was nothing short of a practice match as they conceded 544 against the Cricket Australia XI team. They also lost their young new talent, Prithvi Shaw, who suffered an ankle injury while fielding.

The contest that started in Adelaide was India's twelfth attempt to win a Test series in Australia since 1948. India were the first Asian team to tour Australia under Lala Amarnath's captaincy in 1947–48. Their record in Australia, which started with a crushing series loss to Don Bradman's side in 1948, was five wins from forty-four Tests and drawn series in 1980–81, 1985–86, and 2003–04. Now in 2018, Virat had a great record on this ground, and before this match, he averaged 98.50 with three centuries there.

India beat Australia by 31 runs in the first Test and led the four-match series 1–0. It was their first victory on Australian soil in a decade, and only their sixth in seventy years. With 191 runs in the first innings and a half-century in the second, Cheteshwar Pujara helped India sail past the Aussies.

Virat wasn't far behind, becoming the fastest to score 1,000 Test runs for India in Australia. He surpassed Sir Donald Bradman's milestone by reaching the figure in nine matches while the latter reached the four-figure mark in his tenth Test at home.

Australia bounced back to claim the second Test in Perth by 146 runs in a classic team effort, which made Virat's century in the first innings go waste. It was his sixth hundred in Australia but he was in no mood to discuss it. He also became the second fastest to twenty-five Test hundreds after Bradman, but he said it was irrelevant because India had lost. The four-match Test series was levelled at 1–1.

The third Test started on the Boxing Day at the Melbourne Cricket Ground. Australia began the final day on 258–8 chasing the target of 399. India just took 4.3 overs to wrap up their win and had an unassailable 2–1 lead in the four-match Test series, thereby retaining the Border–Gavaskar Trophy!

'Credit has to go to the bowlers,' Virat said. 'I think they have been outstanding, especially Jasprit [Bumrah]... Nothing is going to distract us from ... winning that last Test match.'[49] With this win, Virat equalled Sourav Ganguly's record of most wins on foreign soil.

Most Wins in Overseas Tests as Captain (India)

Wins	Captain	Matches
11	**Virat Kohli**	24
11	Sourav Ganguly	28
06	M.S. Dhoni	30
05	Rahul Dravid	17

This match victory left India in the reckoning for their first-ever series win in Australia, with one more Test to go at Sydney Cricket Ground. Here, the Indian team was once again in a dominant position before rain robbed them of a 3–1 finish. The fourth Test was officially abandoned on the final day, and India had to be content with a score of 2–1. It was a historic series victory Down Under and India became the first visiting team in thirty years to enforce a follow-on against Australia. India also became the first team from the subcontinent to conquer Australia on their home soil.

For Virat, it had taken nearly a year and three of the toughest tours to shed the tag of 'poor travellers' stuck to the Indian team, who tended to lose matches abroad.

'A very proud moment,' Virat said at the presentation. 'More so because for the last twelve months we understand what we have gone through as a team, we understand the kind of cricket we have been able to play. But the fact that the reward has come in the most historic series for Indian cricket is the cherry on the top of the cake.'[50]

The 'Little Master' Sunil Gavaskar could not hold back his tears after watching the Indian team lift the trophy. 'I was very proud seeing India lift the trophy. I had tears in my eyes because this is a historic moment.'[51]

This win made Virat one of the greatest players the game has ever seen and the best of his time. Australia was Virat's fourth series win after taking over the captaincy from M.S. Dhoni. '...I've never been more proud of being part of a team,' Virat said. 'By far, this is my biggest achievement. The series win will give us a different identity.'[52]

Series Wins Away from Home for Virat

Score	Venue	Year
2–1	Sri Lanka	2015
2–0	West Indies	2016
3–0	Sri Lanka	2017
2–1	Australia	2018–19

The India versus Australia series was a landmark Test series won after seventy-two years, thirty-one series, ninety-eight Tests, 292 players and twenty-nine captains! Virat's former teammate Ashish Nehra was all praise for him. 'Four years back and now – Virat is a different player. See his Melbourne innings with Pujara; he has changed his game – see how he played against Jimmy Anderson. He has scored on every ground and against every country. He is very consistent.'

However, for Captain Kohli this series was more about his leadership rather than his batting. His bowling changes were spot on. He showed that he only plays to win a match.

Cricket World Cup 2019

Team India is gearing up to switch formats to T20. The biggest assignment for them and their captain Virat is the 2019 World Cup in England, where he will attempt to become the third Indian skipper to win the 50-over mega-event after Kapil Dev (1983) and M.S. Dhoni (2011).

Michael Clarke believes that this World Cup is very important for Virat as a captain. 'He handles pressure perfectly and he always looks forward to perform on the big stage like the World Cup,' says Clarke. 'If Virat is in your team, it's very hard to write that team off.'

A World Cup triumph after eight years would cement Virat's legacy as one of the greatest captains India has ever had. All the best!

 **As Test captain, Virat's win percentage is the highest among Indian skippers.**

18

The boy who broke and set records

Virat, the latest greatest run machine of India, has been breaking records left, right and centre over the last few years, and at an unprecedented pace. Here are some of his most amazing records in Tests, ODIs and T20Is.

Tests

O Virat is the first ever batsman to score double hundreds in four consecutive Test series. He achieved the feat against West Indies, New Zealand, England and Bangladesh in 2016–17. This is the longest such sequence with which he went past cricket greats Rahul

Dravid and Don Bradman, who have done it in three back-to-back series.

○ He is the first batsman in the world to score three double centuries each in successive calendar years (2016 and 2017), against West Indies, New Zealand, England and Bangladesh.

○ He scored 610 runs against Sri Lanka in 2017, which is the highest by an Indian in a three-match Test series.

○ His ICC Test rating points of 937 in August 2018 is the highest garnered by any Indian cricketer.

○ Virat beat Australian cricket legend Don Bradman to become the fastest to make 1,000 Test runs in Australia. He reached the landmark in 2018 at Adelaide in nine Test matches, quicker than Bradman, who had reached the four-figure mark in his tenth Test at Brisbane in 1931.

○ He is the first Asian batsmen to score centuries in South Africa, England and Australia in the same year in Test cricket. He achieved this in 2018.

○ Virat Kohli and Sachin Tendulkar are the only two batsmen to score six centuries in Australia in the last 70 years. Virat made his maiden hundred against Australia in that country in 2012 at Adelaide and over the course of the next two outings Down Under, Virat has carved five more centuries equal Sachin. Tendulkar took 20 Tests to reach the mark and Virat needed only 10 Tests. Virat scored his sixth century in

2018. West Indian Clive Lloyd, and England players Alastair Cook and David Gower, all have five centuries each in Australia.

Most Centuries by a Visiting Batsman in Australia

Player	Match	Centuries
Sir Jack Hobbs (ENG)	24	9
Wally Hammond (ENG)	19	7
Virat Kohli (IND)	10	6
Herbert Sutcliffe (ENG)	14	6
Sachin Tendulkar (IND)	20	6

O Virat reached 25 Test hundreds in 127 innings at Perth in 2018, second to Don Bradman who completed the feat in 68 innings against India at Melbourne in 1948. Sachin Tendulkar is third on the list, having made his 25 Test hundreds in 130 innings.

Fastest to 25 Centuries (Tests)

Rank	Player	Innings
1	Don Bradman	68
2	**Virat Kohli**	**127**
3	Sachin Tendulkar	130
4	Sunil Gavaskar	138
5	Mathew Hayden	139

○ Virat is third on the list of all-time top scorers in overseas Tests in any calendar year:

Player	Matches	Runs	Year	Countries
Graeme Smith	11	1212	2008	Bangladesh, India, England, Australia
Vivian Richards	7	1154	1976	Australia, England
Virat Kohli	**11**	**1138**	**2018**	**South Africa, England, Australia**
Rahul Dravid	11	1137	2002	West Indies, England, New Zealand
Mohinder Amarnath	9	1065	1983	Pakistan, West Indies

○ Virat was the top scorer in Tests in 2018 among all cricketers in the world.

Leading Test Run Scorers in 2018

Batsman	Mat	Runs	Avg
Virat Kohli (IND)	**13**	**1322**	**55.08**
Kusal Mendis (SL)	12	1023	46.50
Joe Root (ENG)	13	948	41.21

| Cheteshwar Pujara (IND) | 13 | 837 | 38.46 |
| Jos Buttler (ENG) | 10 | 760 | 44.70 |

Captaincy – Tests

○ Virat is credited with having won the most consecutive Test series as captain. Between 2015 and 2017, he won nine consecutive series equalling Ricky Ponting's record made during 2005–08.

○ He became the first Asian captain to register Test wins in Australia, England and South Africa in the same calendar year (2018).

○ Virat became the first Test player to register three centuries in his first three innings as a Test captain, during the 2014–15 season. He achieved this feat against Australia when he followed his twin hundreds at the Adelaide Test with a scintillating 140 at Sydney.

○ Virat Kohli added another feather to his illustrious cap when he guided India to a magnificent 137-run win at the Melbourne Cricket Ground in 2018. With this, he equalled Sourav Ganguly's record of most wins in overseas Tests as India captain during 2000–05.

○ On 5 October 2018, Virat Kohli became the first captain to score 1000+ Test runs in three consecutive years.

○ As Test captain, Virat's win percentage is the highest among Indian skippers:

Captain	Matches	Wins	Win Percentage
Virat Kohli	**25**	**11**	**44.00**
Sourav Ganguly	28	11	39.28
M.S. Dhoni	30	6	20.00
Rahul Dravid	17	5	33.33

○ He has the most 200-plus scores by a Test captain, anywhere in the world, totalling six. The next best is five by Brian Lara.

○ Virat is the only Test captain in the world to aggregate 200 runs in a Test match on ten occasions. The next best is on seven occasions by Brian Lara and Ricky Ponting.

○ He is the only Test captain in international cricket to register four double-centuries in four successive series from 2016 to 2017.

○ Under Virat, India recorded their longest unbeaten streak of 18 matches, going past their previous best of 17 matches. The streak began in 2015 against Sri Lanka and lasted till 2017 when they lost to Australia, their first loss in 19 months.

○ Virat is the quickest to reach 4,000 runs as Test captain in international cricket. He reached the landmark in just 65 innings in September 2018 against England. The next best is that many runs in 71 innings by Brian Lara.

○ In August 2018, playing against England, Virat became the first captain to make 200 runs in a Test match for the tenth time. Brian Lara and Ricky Ponting are next best with seven such performances each.

○ Virat became the first Indian captain to score 2,000 Test runs away from home, in December 2018.

ODIs

○ Virat has the highest historic rating points in ICC rankings, garnered by an Indian batsman, with 911 points. He is just 24 points behind Vivian Richards, who had 935 points in ICC rankings.

ICC Best-Ever ODI Championship Rating

	Rat.	Name	Nat.	Career Best Rating		Date
1	935	Vivian Richards	WI	935	v PAK	02/12/1985
2	931	Zaheer Abbas	PAK	931	v NZ	20/06/1983
3	921	Greg Chappell	AUS	921	v NZ	03/02/1981
4	919	David Gower	ENG	919	v NZ	15/06/1983

5	918	Dean Jones	AUS	918	v WI	09/03/1991
6	**911**	**Virat Kohli**	**IND**	**911**	**v ENG**	**12/07/2018**
7	910	Javed Miandad	PAK	910	v SL	08/10/1987

* Nat.: Nationality

O Virat became the fastest to 10,000 ODI runs in 2018, while playing against the West Indies. He reached the landmark in 205 innings, breaking Sachin Tendulkar's record. Sachin was the first to muster 10,000 ODI runs in 259 innings. Virat Kohli took just 10 years and 68 days to score 10,000 ODI runs, breaking Rahul Dravid's time-based record of 10 years and 317 days.

Fastest to 10,000 Runs

Player	Time	Mat	Inns
Virat Kohli	**10y 67d**	**213**	**205**
Sachin Tendulkar	11y 103d	266	259
Sourav Ganguly	13y 204d	272	263
Ricky Ponting	12y 37d	272	266
Jacques Kallis	13y 14d	286	272

O Virat Kohli became the fastest (in terms of balls faced) batsman in the world to score 10,000 ODI runs. He took just 10,813 balls to score 10,000 ODI runs.

○ He is also the fastest Indian to cross 1,000, 5,000, 6,000 and 7,000 run marks in ODIs. He is the fastest in the world to cross the 8,000 and 9,000 run marks. He crossed the (9,000 run) milestone in 194 innings, and South Africa's A.B. de Villiers is behind him, having taken 11 innings more to achieve that feat.

○ Virat holds the Indian record for scoring the fastest ODI ton. He made his century in only 52 balls against Australia back in 2013 in Jaipur.

○ Chasing a score brings the best in Virat. He has scored 25 centuries while chasing, which is the highest by any batsman in international cricket. He has achieved this in just 102 innings, compared to Sachin Tendulkar, who scored 17 centuries while chasing, in 232 innings.

○ In 2010, Virat became the fastest to score 1,000 ODI runs in a calendar year. He beat Hashim Amla's record of 15 innings to score those runs.

○ He scored his forty-first century in one-day international in the second ODI against Australia in 2019. He now has the most centuries in 50-over games played in India between the two countries. The record was previously held by Sachin Tendulkar.

○ Virat scored over 300 runs in a bilateral ODI series on six different occasions. No other player has done it more than four times. Those who have done it four times are: Rahul Dravid (IND), Quinton de Kock (SA) and Rohit Sharma (IND).

○ In October 2018, Virat became the first Indian to hit 100s in three consecutive innings against two opponents. He compiled three successive, well-built tons against the West Indies at home that year. Back in 2012, Virat smashed three consecutive centuries against a strong Lankan side.

○ He has the second most centuries in overseas conditions. He now has 22 centuries outside India, behind Sachin Tendulkar's 29. He went past Sanath Jayasuriya and Kumar Sangakkara (21 each) with his century in Adelaide, Australia, in January 2019.

○ Virat Kohli tops the list of the highest career batting average reached in ODIs (100+ innings)

Player	Inns	Runs	Average
1. **Virat Kohli**	**219**	**10843**	**59.57**
2. Michael Bevan	196	6912	53.58
3. A.B. de Villiers	218	9577	53.50
4. Joe Root	119	5090	50.90
5. M.S. Dhoni	289	10500	50.72

○ Virat has garnered the most runs in a bilateral ODI series among all cricketers:

Player	Against	Mat	Runs
1. **Virat Kohli**	**vs South Africa (away)**	**6**	**558**
2. Rohit Sharma	vs Australia (home)	6	491
3. George Bailey	vs India (away)	6	478
4. Hamilton Masakadza	vs Kenya (home)	5	467
5. Chris Gayle	vs India (away)	7	455

Captaincy – ODIs

○ Virat is the quickest to 4,000 runs as ODI captain. He also holds the record for being the quickest to 3,000 ODI runs as captain (in 49 innings).

Player	Country	Innings
1. **Virat Kohli**	**IND**	**63**
2. A.B. de Villiers	SA	77
3. M.S. Dhoni	IND	100
4. Sourav Ganguly	IND	103
5. Sanath Jayasuriya	SL	106

○ He has 19 ODI centuries as a captain. He is just three centuries short of Ricky Ponting's record of 22 centuries.

○ Virat is the first captain to hit six ODI hundreds in a calendar year (in 2017).

○ He is also the fastest skipper to cross 1,000 runs, in his 17th innings, when playing against England in 2017, surpassing A.B. de Villiers who took eighteen innings.

T20Is

○ Virat has the most number of 50+ scores in T20Is. He has gone past the 50-run mark on 20 occasions, along with Rohit Sharma.

Most 50s in T20Is

Player	Inns	Runs	50+	Ave
1. **Virat Kohli**	**62**	**2263**	**20**	**50.28**
2. Rohit Sharma	86	2331	20	32.37
3. Martin Guptill	74	2272	16	33.91
4. Chris Gayle	54	1627	15	32.54
5. Brendon McCullum	70	2140	15	35.66

○ He is the first batsman to score more than 600 runs in a calendar year in T20 internationals. He did it in 2016 with an astonishing average of 106.83 and at a strike rate of 140.26, featuring seven 50s.

○ Virat broke the world record for playing the most innings before recording a duck in T20Is. He recorded his maiden T20I duck after 47 innings, playing in his fifty-second T20 international in Guwahati against Australia in 2017.

○ There are only two batsmen in the world who have an average of 50-plus in the T20 format. Virat is currently number two on the list. He is third on the list of the highest run scorers in T20Is.

Most Runs in T20Is

Player	Mat	Inns	Runs	HS	Ave
1. Rohit Sharma	94	86	2331	118	32.37
2. Martin Guptill	76	74	2272	105	33.91
3. **Virat Kohli**	**67**	**62**	**2263**	**90***	**50.28**
4. Shoaib Malik	111	104	2263	75	30.58
5. Brendon McCullum	71	70	2140	123	35.66

Across all formats

○ Virat is the only player in international cricket to average over 50 in all three formats of the game, i.e., Tests, ODIs and T20Is.

○ He has scored 2,735 runs across all formats in 2018 with 11 hundreds.

○ In 2018, he became the fastest captain to reach 8,000 runs in international cricket. He achieved this feat in a match against West Indies in Visakhapatnam, Andhra Pradesh.

○ Virat is third on the list of players with most hundreds across formats:

Player	Inns	Runs	Ave	100s
1. Sachin Tendulkar (IND)	782	34357	48.52	100
2. Ricky Ponting (AUS/ICC)	668	27483	45.95	71
3. Virat Kohli (IND)	**412**	**19719**	**56.34**	**66**
4. Kumar Sangakkara (Asia/ICC/SL)	666	28016	46.77	63
5. Jacques Kallis (Afr/ICC/SA)	617	25534	49.10	62

Virat kissing the ground after scoring his first double hundred in Tests at the Sir Vivian Richards Stadium in Antigua, West Indies, in 2016

Acknowledgements

When my dear friend Vimal Kumar introduced me to Vatsala Kaul Banerjee of Hachette India, I froze for a moment, but his reassurance and complete confidence on my ability as a writer encouraged me to take on this challenge. Another journalist–writer friend Vimal Mohan too believed in me more than I did in myself.

My deep gratitude to

– my parents, who gave me the best gift of all: the freedom of choice. Believe me, it was a big deal in a conservative family in the 1980s and 90s;

– My *bua* (aunt), Late Kusum Mishra, who has been a source of strength throughout my life;

– My wife, Nilu, who has made sure that the responsibility of raising our children Achintya and Aman is an act of joy;

– All the people I have been privileged to have in my life to guide and support me at various stages of my career when I needed them most. Of course, it is tough to name each one of them here, but when they read this they will know that they are the ones who are very close to my heart and have played a crucial role in my life. I am grateful to my family members for their continued support in my life;

- Rajkumar Sharma, Lalchand Rajput, Harbhajan Singh, Ashish Nehra, Chetan Chauhan, Vivian Richards, Michael Clarke and Tanmay Srivastava for their time and inputs;
- Last but not the least, all my friends, batchmates, colleagues and all my English teachers, especially Shankar Dutt sir, whose words of wisdom always inspired me to do better in life.

– Neeraj Jha

Journalist–author Vimal Kumar. and I have three 'half books' together – attempts that we couldn't complete. As this one goes to press, Vimal's role in pushing us on cannot be overstated.

I would like to thank

- our editor Vatsala Kaul Banerjee, who had the patience to tame two cricket gypsies and produce this work in time;
- Prof. Sunetra Sen Narayan at IIMC, who always inspired me to strive for the best; and finally
- my sports editor Sundeep Misra, with whom I have gained most of my understanding of sports.

– Vidhanshu Kumar

Endnotes & Sources

1. As reported on https://cricketaddictor.com/news/virat-kohlis-fathers-day-post-is-winning-the-internet/

2. Interview with LiveMint: 'Virat Kohli's learning pitch' by Rudraneil Sengupta; Updated: 03 Jun 2017, 08:01 PM IST; https://www.livemint.com/Leisure/PVxATbs5tnJmigJl2r39QO/Virat-Kohlis-learning-pitch.html

3. As reported on https://www.wisden.com/stories/interviews/virat-kohli-exclusive-interview

4. As reported on http://www.espn.in/cricket/story/_/id/22993333/lalchand-rajput-please-19-tour; https://www.ballebaazi.com/blog/virat-kohli-the-evolution/; https://www.outlookindia.com/newswire/story/rajput-pleased-with-under-19-boys-show/406224

5. https://www.telegraphindia.com/entertainment/king-nbsp-of-the-world/cid/1423279; and

6. From an interview with Saroj Kohli in *The Times of India*: 'Virat changed after his dad's death: Mother' by Arghya Ganguly; https://timesofindia.indiatimes.com/sports/new-zealand-in-india-2016/top-stories/Virat-changed-after-his-dads-death-Mother/articleshow/2835049.cms

7. As reported by rediff.com: https://www.rediff.com/cricket/report/kohli-on-his-late-fathers-influence-tendulkar-and-indo-pak-cricket-pix/20160506.htm

8. As reported in *Mid-day*: https://www.mid-day.com/articles/the-ton-will-give-me-a-lot-of-confidence-kohli/99161 and ESPN: http://www.espncricinfo.com/india-v-australia-2010/content/story/482917.html

9. As reported on ESPN: http://www.espncricinfo.com/india-v-australia-2010/content/story/482917.html; The Daily Star: https://www.thedailystar.net/news-detail-159438; NDTV Sports: https://

sports.ndtv.com/cricket/virat-kohli-says-the-ton-will-give-him-a-lot-of-confidence-1588171

10. As reported in *India Today*: https://www.indiatoday.in/sports/world-cup-2011/story/kohli-has-edge-over-raina-for-number-four-slot-at-world-cup-says-dhoni-128805-2011-02-17 and on rediff.com: https://www.rediff.com/cricket/report/slide-show-1-world-cup-2011-kohli-has-edge-over-raina-for-number-four-slot-dhoni/20110217.htm; *The Hindu*: https://www.thehindu.com/sport/Dhoni-gives-Kohli-the-edge-over-Raina-in-lsquoslot-warrsquo/article15448109.ece; India Today: https://www.indiatoday.in/sports/world-cup-2011/story/kohli-has-edge-over-raina-for-number-four-slot-at-world-cup-says-dhoni-128805-2011-02-17; rediff.com: https://www.rediff.com/cricket/report/slide-show-world-cup-2011-video-dhoni-virat-kohli-suresh-raina/20110217.htm; *Jagran Post*: http://post.jagran.com/dhoni-favours-inform-kohli-over-raina-1297925144; *Times of India*: https://timesofindia.indiatimes.com/news/India-seek-revenge-against-Bangladesh-in-World-Cup-opener/articleshow/7521335.cms

11. As reported on TimesNowNews.com: https://www.timesnownews.com/sports/cricket/ipl/article/virat-kohlis-development-as-a-great-from-the-eyes-gary-kirsten-under-whom-he-made-odi-debut/219001; *Times of India*: https://timesofindia.indiatimes.com/sports/cricket/ipl/top-stories/virat-kohli-always-had-the-hunger-to-be-great-gary-kirsten/articleshow/63824730.cms; *The Indian Express*: https://indianexpress.com/article/sports/ipl/ipl-2018-any-guy-with-half-a-cricket-eye-would-have-known-virat-kohli-was-going-to-be-a-great-player-reveals-gary-kirsten-5143940/; Circle of Cricket: https://circleofcricket.com/category/IPL_2018/19979/ipl-2018-virat-kohli-was-destined-for-greatness-says-gary-kirsten; Scroll.in: https://scroll.in/field/876179/virat-kohli-has-gone-from-the-prodigious-talent-to-the-high-performer-gary-kirsten

12. As featured on Sportskeeda: https://www.sportskeeda.com/cricket/great-opportunity-for-india-to-do-world-cup-double-virat-kohli

13. As reported on BCCI.TV: http://www.bcci.tv/news/2015/features-and-interviews/10103/virat-kohlis-life-between-two-world-cups

14. As reported on ABC News: https://www.abc.net.au/news/2012-01-26/kohli-stands-tall-on-australia27s-day/3795350

15. As reported on: https://www.cricketcountry.com/news/dean-jones-likens-virat-kohli-s-century-to-viv-richards-epic-knock-11987.

16. and 17. *Mumbai Mirror*: https://mumbaimirror.indiatimes.com/sport/cricket/virat-a-lot-like-me-viv-richards/articleshow/19736923.cms; *The Free Press Journal*: https://www.freepressjournal.in/sports/virat-reminds-me-of-myself-richards/178095; IndianCricketFans.com: http://img.khelnama.com/130425/cricket/news/virat-kohli-reminds-me-myself-says-vivian-richards/8540

18. As reported on NDTV Sports: https://sports.ndtv.com/south-africa-vs-india-2013-14/virat-kohli-reminded-me-of-sachin-tendulkar-says-allan-donald-1525835

19. As featured on Direct Hit: https://www.directhit.com.au/glenn-maxwell/news/2018/ 10/24/best-in-the-world-maxi-on-kohli

20. As reported on: https://m.dailyhunt.in/news/india/english/sportzwiki+english-epaper-sptwiken/it+s+flattering+to+be+compared+to+virat+kohli+babar+azam-newsid-109413457; https://www.icc-cricket.com/womens-world-cup/news/1059021

21. As reported on: https://www.skysports.com/cricket/news/12344/11423032/what-makes-virat-kohli-great-we-asked-the-sky-sports-cricket-experts-ahead-of-england-v-india; https://circleofcricket.com/category/ENG_v_IND_2018/23684/eng-v-ind-2018-england-cricket-experts-share-their-view-on-virat-kohli

22. As reported on: https://www.theguardian.com/sport/blog/2018/aug/29/joe-root-virat-kohli-five-fourth-test-pointers-england-india-ageas-bowl

23. Quoted on various sites

24. As reported on CricketCountry: https://www.cricketcountry.com/news/virat-kohli-states-nothing-can-affect-his-friendship-with-ms-dhoni-657610; NDTV Sports: https://sports.ndtv.com/cricket/some-tried-to-create-a-rift-between-ms-dhoni-and-me-virat-kohli-1771417

25. As reported on: https://twitter.com/ashwinravi99/status/714306738111942657

26. As reported on: https://www.indiatoday.in/sports/cricket/story/virat-kohli-will-go-down-with-viv-richards-as-one-of-the-greatest-ever-in-odis-warne-1453117-2019-02-11; https://www.outlookindia.com/website/

story/sports-news-shane-warne-will-wait-to-see-if-virat-kohli-is-the-greatest-batsman-ever/325351; https://www.cricketcountry.com/news/very-hard-to-judge-eras-shane-warne-on-virat-kohli-sachin-tendulkar-comparison-801927

27. As reported on: https://www.telegraph.co.uk/cricket/2016/11/22/virat-kohli-interview-people-think-superman-michael-vaughan/; https://zeenews.india.com/cricket/virat-kohlis-interview-with-michael-vaughan-fitness-drinks-parties-milestones-and-other-best-picks_1952638.html

28. As reported on: https://www.theguardian.com/sport/blog/2009/oct/28/india-australia-one-day-series

29. As reported on: https://www.google.com/search?rlz=1C1NHXL_enIN802IN802&q=%E2%80%98Throughout+the+history+of+Indian+cricket,+fielding+has+been+very+poor.+We+didn%27t+have+the+grounds+to+learn+fielding.+We+don%E2%80%99t+know+how+to+dive;+we+don%E2%80%99t+know+how+to+slide+because+we+don%E2%80%99t+have+such+ground+where+we+can+slide+on.%E2%80%991&spell=1&sa=X&ved=0ahUKEwiZ4KqR3bvhAhUY7HMBHSSZDPUQBQgrKAA&biw=1101&bih=544

30. As reported on: https://www.deccanherald.com/content/582501/when-duncan-checked-kohli-understood.html; https://www.newsnation.in/article/151854-former-india-coach-duncan-fletcher-helped-virat-kohli-understand-the-value-of-fitness.html

31. & 32. As reported on: https://www.cricketcountry.com/news/virat-kohli-duncan-fletcher-told-me-that-cricket-is-the-most-unprofessional-of-professional-sports-549894

33. As reported on: https://www.firstpost.com/sports/100-squats-weight-lifting-virat-kohli-reveals-his-fitness-regime-2798824.html; https://metrosaga.com/workout-and-diet-plan-of-virat-kohli/

34. As reported on: https://www.news18.com/cricketnext/news/ajinkya-rahane-follows-skipper-virat-kohli-to-the-gym-1345038.html; https://www.deccanherald.com/content/582501/when-duncan-checked-kohli-understood.html

35. As reported on: https://m.dailyhunt.in/news/india/english/deccan+chronicle-epaper-deccanch/here+s+what+virat+kohli+eats+for+breakfast+lunch+and+dinner+and+his+fitness+regime-newsid-81413204;

https://timesofindia.indiatimes.com/sports/cricket/india-in-south-africa/virat-kohli-says-he-wants-to-play-with-same-energy-even-when-hes-35/articleshow/62844597.cms

36. https://www.scoopwhoop.com/things-we-learnt-virat-kohlis-breakfast-with-champions/;

37. https://www.indiatoday.in/cricket/story/cricket-virat-kohli-mens-health-magazine-114926-2012-09-01

38. https://www.ndtv.com/health/india-vs-pak-5-things-virat-kohli-is-doing-to-score-a-century-diet-and-exercise-tips-1713681; https://witv.atavist.com/revealed-secrets-of-virat-kholis-fitness-

39. LiveMint: https://www.livemint.com/Consumer/dZMTVU0L1uHA11Oe Mmbrfl/Virat-Kohli-set-to-become-a-Rs100-crore-brand.html

40. As reported on: https://economictimes.indiatimes.com/industry/services/advertising/brand-kohli-steadily-on-the-rise-after-2012-bats-for-over-3-hours-a-day-on-tv/articleshow/57611022.cms?from=mdr; https://thesportsrush.com/rise-rise-brand-virat-kohli/; https://www.exchange4media.com/media-tv-news/tam-ad-volume-data-shows-18growth-on-tv-in-first-six-months-of-2018-92140.html

41. ESPN.com: http://www.espn.com/espn/feature/story/_/page/WorldFame/espn-world-fame-100-2018

42. Forbes India: http://www.forbesindia.com/lists/2018-celebrity-100/1735/1

43. As reported on: http://www.mondaq.com/india/x/771508/Social+Media/Duff+Phelps+Launches+Celebrity+Brand+Valuation+Report+2018

44. As reported in *Deccan Chronicle*: https://www.deccanchronicle.com/sports/cricket/270516/i-see-every-day-as-a-new-day-virat-kohli-on-his-dream-run.html; rediff.com: https://www.rediff.com/cricket/report/no-substitute-to-hard-work-and-discipline-kohli/20160527.htm

45. As reported on: https://www.firstpost.com/sports/focus-aggression-motivation-and-vision-kohli-on-what-makes-kohli-2279104.html; sourced from: interview in *ESPNCricinfo Cricket Monthly*

46. As reported in *Afternoon Voice*: https://www.afternoonvoice.com/not-proud-of-the-way-weve-played-we-deserved-to-lose-this-game-kohli.html; *Hindustan Times*: https://www.hindustantimes.com/cricket/india-

vs-england-we-deserved-to-lose-virat-kohli-after-lord-s-test-defeat/story-1fz7NolD4p2ugLWpLu8GcK.html

47. As told to Neeraj Jha

48. As reported on Scroll.in: https://scroll.in/field/905173/despite-adelaide-test-win-india-need-to-step-up-as-a-batting-group-says-virat-kohli

49. Reported in *Hindustan Times*: https://www.hindustantimes.com/cricket/india-vs-australia-virat-kohli-reveals-secret-behind-bumrah-success/story-mZokrTloEwwBDRwZMoTuIJ.html; Daily Star: https://www.thedailystar.net/sports/cricket/news/be-scared-bumrah-kohli-1680904

50. As reported on: https://www.cricketcountry.com/news/india-vs-australia-series-win-12-months-in-making-says-very-proud-virat-kohli-788350; https://cricshots.com/virat-kohli-team-effort-win-historic-test-series-australia/; http://sumod-sunny-joseph.blogspot.com/2019/01/india-cricket-captain-virat-kohli-and.html

51. As reported in *India Today*: https://www.indiatoday.in/sports/cricket/story/sunil-gavaskar-india-vs-australia-border-gavaskar-trophy-sydney-cheteshwar-pujara-1425675-2019-01-07; Hindustan Times: https://www.hindustantimes.com/cricket/india-vs-australia-virat-kohli-lifting-trophy-brought-tears-to-sunil-gavaskar-s-eyes/story-GtWQevuRGBxPd8BTKu6t8L.html

52. As reported on CricTracker: https://www.crictracker.com/ive-never-been-more-proud-of-a-team-than-this-one-virat-kohli/; The Quint: https://www.thequint.com/sports/cricket/watch-virat-kohli-emotional-speech-after-india-win-first-ever-test-series-in-australia; Cricket Country: https://www.cricketcountry.com/news/india-vs-australia-4th-test-never-been-more-proud-of-a-team-than-this-one-virat-kohli-788263

* All accessed in March 2019; Shorter quotes are from various sources.